Quilts Across America

Fig. 1. New York—The National Needlework Association

Also by Leslie Linsley:

The Weekend Quilt
First Steps in Counted Cross Stitch
First Steps in Stenciling
First Steps in Quilting
Carry-Along Crochet
Country Decorating with Fabric Crafts
Night Before Christmas Craft Book
Christmas Ornaments and Stockings
America's Favorite Quilts
Million Dollar Projects from the 5 & 10¢ Store
Making It Personal
The Great Bazaar
Army/Navy Surplus: A Decorating Source
Afghans to Knit and Crochet
Quick and Easy Knit and Crochet
Custom Made
Wildcrafts
The Decoupage Workshop
Decoupage: A New Look at an Old Craft
Decoupage for Young Crafters
Air Crafts
Fabulous Furniture Decorations
New Ideas for Old Furniture
Photocrafts
Scrimshaw

Quilts Across America

The Making of the Great American Quilt Banner

Leslie Linsley

with The National Needlework Association

St. Martin's Press

New York

Preparation and design: Jon Aron Studio

Project director: Robby Smith
Illustrations: Peter Peluso, Jr.
Robby Smith
Photography: Picture Archives, Jerry Palubniak

Design by Jon Aron

Library of Congress Cataloging-in-Publication Data

Linsley, Leslie.
   Quilts across America / Leslie Linsley.
     p. cm.
   ISBN 0-312-01437-6 : $22.95
   1. Quilting—Patterns. 2. Quilts—United States. I. Title.
  TT835.L5654 1988
   746.9'7'0973—dc 19   87-27112
                         CIP

First Edition
10 9 8 7 6 5 4 3 2 1

Contents

Fig. 2. New York—Janet Page-Kessler

Quilts Across America

Fig. 3. Maine—Maureen Heath

The Great American Quilt Banner

It all started with the Statue of Liberty. A birthday party was in the making for the centennial celebration in New York harbor. One of the major events being planned was The Great American Quilt Festival, which would focus people's attention on the art of quilting through a national contest. This event was to take place at the exhibition pier in New York City.

And then there was the phone call that set in motion one of the greatest, all-out, grass-roots efforts this country has ever seen. It was early fall and the call came from the American Folk Museum festival committee to Mary Colucci, executive director of The National Needlework Association (TNNA), representing the nation's needlecraft industry. The proposed project was so overwhelming in scope that it took a while to sink in as a real possibility for the small TNNA staff. What they were asked to do was coordinate the execution of a thousand-foot-long quilted banner that would represent every state in the Union from Maine to Hawaii. The banner would be the focal point of The Great American Quilt Festival.

Once they caught their breath, the TNNA staff set about the task of finding quilters able and willing to participate in representing their state. How does one small group of women organize such a gigantic job? They began by writing dozens of letters, making hundreds of phone calls, and contacting local stores, homemakers' groups, and quilting clubs all over the country in an effort to find people willing to donate a three-foot-square quilted section for this banner.

Next, they created a registration form to be completed by group members who were interested in being part of this project. Each person or group was asked to submit a design idea for consideration. The theme was to be one that would best represent the state in which the quilters lived. This could be an historic event, person, or place. It might be the state's flower or bird or a particular state building. It could be several points of interest or the shape of the state. The techniques were to be patchwork and appliqué, and each square could be machine- or hand-quilted. Once the design ideas were approved, making sure that there weren't too many duplications, the quilters would be sent another form. This would be for the purpose of gathering information about the people involved in the project, who would be asked to fill in facts about why they chose a particular design and what materials they used to make their quilts. Further, they were asked to give some personal information such as their ages, where they learned to quilt, did anyone else in the family quilt, when did they begin quilting and why. They were also encouraged to share anecdotes about their quilting experiences.

These fact sheets would then be used by TNNA to keep track of which states were contributing and which were falling behind. If someone registered his or her design, for example, and it was accepted, the staff was then counting on receiving that square by a determined deadline. At one point, Lois Nash, a TNNA staffer announced, "New England states are doing fine. We'll have to put a fire under the Midwest."

The information about each quilter would later be used to inform others, through a newsletter, about the people who were contributing hundreds of hours to the whole project. In this way, a quilter working alone in Alaska, for example, would know that there was a quilter in Hawaii working on a similar project at the same time. And while each person was working on a complete square, each square would become part of a whole project that would become the banner. This exchange created a unified project, with all participants working on part of the banner but feeling involved in the whole as well. It made for a connection during isolated quilting hours and added to the patriotic spirit of the event.

At the same time, The Fineberg Publicity firm for TNNA was sending notices to local newspapers telling about area residents or clubs that were participating. This created interest all over the country. The *Goshen News* in Indiana was one such paper to write an article about three local women—*Marie Cross*, her daughter *Pat Hochstedler*, and her daughter-in-law *Mary Ann Lienhart-Cross*—who spent thirty-two hours cutting, sewing, and quilting their section. Their banner part included a farm scene, a horse and buggy, Bonneyville Mill, and the state capitol, to give a total picture of northern Indiana. The pattern pieces were machine appliquéd and the hand-quilting was done on a hundred-year-old frame belonging to Mary Ann's grandmother, who had quilted all her life.

The *Idaho Enterprise* ran a story on the Oneida County Extension Homemaker's Council members. Pictured holding their entry were *Helen McDaniel*, president; *Shirley Grubb*; and *Glenda Jensen*. Their block illustrated the Lewis and Clark Expedition and Oregon Trail. A lot of hours went into the quilt and many women worked on different parts of it, creating a very tight-knit group of dedicated women.

Each month TNNA's newsletter, "Banner Headlines," gave up-to-date news on the progress of the banner. By Christmas they had received almost one hundred registration forms. But, in order to create a banner one thousand feet long, approximately 350 sections would be needed, or an average of seven sections per state. Only three states hadn't yet sent in their forms—Alaska, Delaware, and Utah—but TNNA was hopeful that at least one person from each of these states would respond shortly. And it was important that every state be represented.

For weeks the office was quiet. Mary Rauch said, "I sure hope this is a sign that everyone's quilting out there." And then one day a box arrived with the first quilt. It was a cause for celebration at The National Needlework Association. They were on their way. Days and sometimes weeks went by without any response. Mary and her staff were on the phone again, calling to find out how the projects were coming along. Soon the United Parcel Service man was making daily deliveries and things picked up around the office. It was like having a birthday every day. "I wonder which states will arrive today," said Ken, who mans the phones and greets visitors, including the very welcome UPS man.

The first three quilt squares couldn't have been more diverse. From the state of Idaho came a quilt from *Willa Caldwell* of Wendell. Through her fact sheet we learned that she was 92 and had two great-great-grandchildren. Her square was a bright gold map of Idaho with a blue background. It showed points of interest and prod-

Fig. 4. Maine—Judy Babbidge

Fig. 5. Maine—Marjorie W. Capen

Fig. 6. New Hampshire—Pam Pearson, Julie Goddard, Marcia Good-now, Janis Hancock, Jessie McKone, and Wanda Jewett

13

ucts in the state. She has been a member of Extension Homemakers for years and is a former president for her county. Her mother taught her to quilt more than seventy-five years ago. What a wonderful heritage passed on to her family!

At the other end of the spectrum came a banner square from a fifth-grade class at St. Francis School in Goshen, Kentucky. Under the leadership of their teacher, *Gillian Ames,* these ten-year-olds each made a six-inch square block using appliqué and embroidery techniques. The squares were then joined and a border added to make the 3-×-3-foot section. Each small block was used to feature various things related to Kentucky—a spinning wheel; an ore cart from mining operations; a cardinal, which is the state bird; and a southern belle with parasol. The students quilted sections of the piece in a design suggesting the headdress of the Statue of Liberty.

Patty Codopony sent her quilt from Binger, Oklahoma. Her description of her design and why she chose it is probably one of the loveliest that came into the TNNA office. "My quilted section is dedicated to my husband and sons in honor of their noble heritage." She wrote. "The theme I selected for my quilt square is the relationship of Oklahoma with the Plains Indians. Shown around the outline of the state are the horse and buffalo, the two animals that brought the Plains Indians to the height of their power. The tail of the horse is formed with hair from my own horse's tail. This theme not only symbolizes my state, it is also personally significant since my husband and two sons are Kiowa/Comanche. I have also included the shields from these two tribes, acknowledged as being among the best horsemen and hunters on the plains, if not the world . . ."

These letters gave the quilts more meaning. They had been stitched by real people from diverse backgrounds, yet all of them shared this one common interest.

"Let's make the banner come alive for everyone who sees it," Mary Colucci suggested. And so the next issue of "Banner Headlines" asked that all quilters send a recent snapshot taken while working on their quilts. The plan was to make a photo montage to display at the festival. In this way those who viewed the banner could see all the people who made it a reality.

By the middle of January, fifty quilt squares had been delivered from all parts of the United States, even a quilt from Guam. The quality of the work and the creativity of design were impressive, but now what TNNA needed most was quantity.

The conference room was beginning to fill up. Sheets of paper representing each state were taped around the room. Under the state's name was a list of quilt makers. On the floor, under these lists, were the neatly folded quilt squares from the individual states. When a state didn't have any entries, one of the staff was on the phone once again. "Where are your quilts? We need you." And so it progressed with the March deadline looming.

While coordinating the completion of the banner, TNNA's group of dedicated workers got bitten by the quilting bug. It crept over them slowly, hitting one, then another, until it was unanimously decided that they had to make a section themselves. They chose the red, white, and blue banner logo and it became the first sec-

Fig. 7. New Hampshire—The Cochico Quilters Guild

Fig. 8. New Hampshire—The Deerfield/Epping Quilters

Fig. 9. New Hampshire—Country Roads Quilt Guild

tion of the banner (Figure 1), followed by the Statue of Liberty square (Figure 2). The Statue of Liberty quilt, made by *Janet Page-Kessler* for Ameritex, was 100 percent cotton and stenciled with fabric paint. Janet learned to quilt from her grandmother, who taught her English paper piecing at age ten. She is a professional quilter for two major fabric companies.

As the banner took shape, plans were made for displaying it at The Great American Quilt Festival to be held in April. It was decided that all sections from one state would be joined together and placed next to the states in the same region of the country. The banner would read from the East Coast to the West and be hung from a wire strung the length of the interior of the exhibition hall. Because of its size and location and the placement just above head height, nobody could miss it.

The banner was becoming a reality. Each day's mail brought batches of letters about the quilters. *Margaret Bishop Brehmer* from Sag Harbor, New York, was born in 1928. She learned to quilt in 1955 and had been planning a patriotic theme for a long time. She loves the words of "America the Beautiful," some of which were used in her quilt. Margaret's mother was an avid needleperson, as is her sister. In fact, together with her sister and *Jean DeVed Chivers,* she completed a sesquicentennial quilt for Mt. Holyoke College in Massachusetts. Margaret is a member of several quilt groups and the assistant editor of Long Island Quilter's Guild Newsletter.

The first quilt from Maine came from *Maureen Heath* of Sedgwick, and it is called "The Sun Rises First in Maine" (Figure 3). "Sunrise occurs along the Maine coast sooner than anywhere else in the United States," Mrs. Heath wrote. "Depending on the season of the year 'first' sunrise can be in either West Quoddy Head, Mount Katahdin, Mars Hills, or Cadillac Mountain." This was her first quilt and she planned the theme, assembled the materials, and learned how to do it in ten days! Because she lives twenty-five miles from a fabric store, getting the materials was the most difficult and the choices were limited. In the middle of a snowstorm, Maureen's husband drove fifteen miles to get more thread and fixed her sewing machine just in the nick of time. Why did she do it? "I wanted to be involved in a personal way with the Statue of Liberty centennial celebrations. Many years ago my mother and father came from Ireland to this country through Ellis Island. Years later I was returning from a European tour of duty with the United States Navy. Sailing into New York Harbor past The Lady, I felt what thousands of immigrants must have experienced . . . that this was home. And now I was also able to brag about my adopted home, Maine." She did put her age on the fact sheet but said, "You should never ask a lady her age."

Judy Babbidge is from Stockholm, Maine. Her square took sixty hours and she worked alone. "February in northern Maine is the perfect time to hibernate and create a quilt," she said. Her quilt square is all patchwork, representing the four seasons enjoyed in her state (Figure 4). The center block represents the Pine Tree State. The small corner blocks represent the seasons: flower garden path for spring, sunshiny day for summer, autumn leaf for fall, and snowball for

Fig. 10. New Hampshire—Joann Bailey, Doris Pike, and Anne White

winter. This is a design that anyone might enjoy re-creating. Judy used only cotton and ecology cloth. She has been quilting for four years and still hasn't finished the first quilt she started! Her love of quilting comes from fond memories of childhood days spent with friends while their mothers made quilts to raise money for the church. To make this quilt, see page 120.

A breathtaking example of appliqué and hand-quilting came from *Marjorie W. Capen* of Deer Isle, Maine (Figure 5). The simplicity of a down-east windjammer, the *Stephen Taber,* sailing on the cool blue water of the Penobscot Bay is offset by the Camden Hills in the background. Sea gulls add a nice touch overhead. One can almost hear their squawks. See page 124 for quilt design.

Fortunately for the banner committee, it was still the dead of winter, a good time for quilting in Maine, and from Bucksport came another entry just one week before deadline. *Terry Swazey,* her mother, *June Curtis,* a helper, *Lorraine Sullivan,* and four of their children worked together. Their theme was Maine black bears. Terry has been quilting since she was a teenager. Her mother learned from a friend, which led to many friends forming a quilting bee, and they became the first to join the State Pine Tree Quilter's Guild. They quilt for relaxation and because they love quilts.

Margaret M. Jones of Caribou, Maine, is also proud of her state, which she appliquéd on her square. Maine's potato, blueberry, lobster, fishing, hunting, and skiing industries were represented, along with trees, the state bird (chickadee), and the state flower (white pine-cone and tassel). Born in northern Maine, Mar-

garet has been married thirty years and has two sons. She enjoys all types of needlework and has taught others for five years. Her business, Margie's Patchwork Heaven, specializes in quilting supplies and fabrics.

Mary Elwell of Wilton, Maine, has always lived in that rural area. She is the oldest in a family of eleven and is proud of her state. She says, "As I've grown through the years, I am more appreciative of the beauty and pleasure of living and raising my four children here. My husband and I have been apple growers for over thirty years and rely on the environment and its elements." Her quilt was made to represent the wonderful vacation aspects that Maine has to offer.

One day while viewing a group of quilt squares and reading some of the mail, Mary Colucci was moved to reflect, "This project truly celebrates the wonderful qualities of needlecrafting. Quilting is a needleart technique that expresses our past, tying together the threads of family, history, and the arts. *From Sea to Shining Sea* is a national endeavor, saluting America and an American tradition—needleart. Just read some of these," she said, passing the letters to the others.

"Six of us are members of a Quilt of the Month group. We love handcrafts and meet once a month to assemble a quilt and to socialize," wrote *Pam Pearson* of Dover, New Hampshire. Along with *Julie Goddard, Marcia Goodnow, Janis Hancock, Jessie McKone,* and *Wanda Jewett,* she designed and swapped fabric for each block of their banner square. During that time one of them had a baby, all were going away on vacation for a total of twenty-nine days, and yet they completed the square in one month. Their quilt

Fig. 11. New Hampshire—Sandra Hatch, Ruth Swasey, and Gloria Cosgrove

Fig. 12. Massachusetts—The Cranberry Quilters

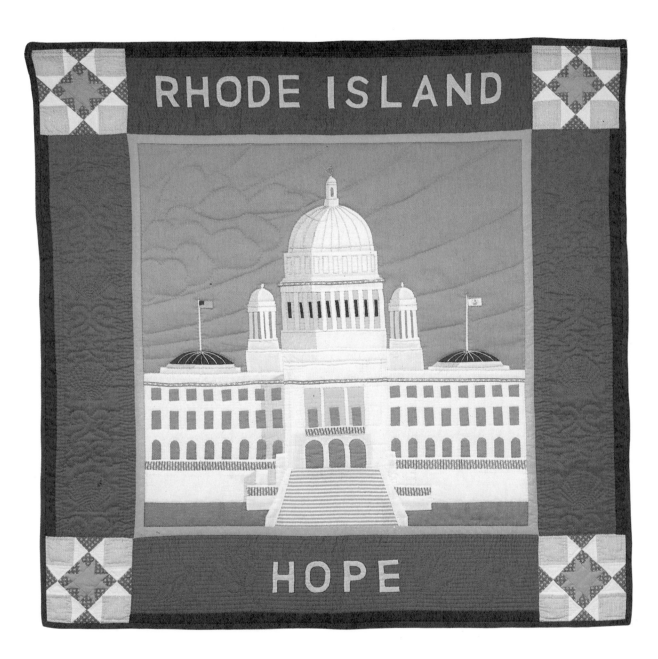

Fig. 13. Rhode Island—Deborah S. King

shows four different covered bridges in the four seasons of New Hampshire (Figure 6). See page 125 for quilt design.

Linda K. Scherf is another Dover resident who worked with ten members of the Cochico Quilters Guild (Figure 7). "Being a native of New Hampshire, my family went each summer to the White Mountains, where the granite rocks are so beautiful," she wrote. "We all used one fabric within every square to tie them together. The banner section is scrapbag." All the guild members learned to sew at an early age from their mothers or grandmothers. *Nancy Hubbard* wrote that she has a very understanding husband (most of the time). Ever since she took a course she has been consumed by quilting. "I am constantly being challenged and delighted with the art."

Many of the banner participants learned to sew as children and have found constant satisfaction from this endeavor. Although they are busy homemakers, some with children and businesses or jobs, they all find time for their needlearts. Often the letters revealed two, three, and sometimes four generations of quilters in a family. Those first-generation stitchers expressed a desire to pass along their knowledge and enthusiasm to their children, thus continuing a long-established American tradition. *Louise Ford* of South Berwick, Maine, wrote, "After enrolling in a quilting class ten years ago, I made four quilts. I have a sister who quilts and a few years ago we talked our eighty-year-old mother into making her first quilt. She is just finishing her second quilt and her older sister has just completed her first quilt top made entirely by hand. Quilting is contagious!"

Betty Lou Cassidy of Linwood, New Jersey, teaches first through fourth grades at a Learning Resource Center. She learned to quilt after taking a Mariner's Compass Workshop. "My grandmothers both quilted. I began stitching in the fifth grade and feel strongly that a true love of needlework begins in childhood."

"I am fifty-eight and learned to quilt at age five," wrote *Zolalee Gaylor* of Midwest City, Oklahoma. "My mother quilted into her eighties and I inherited her love. I have dozens of quilts running around in my head. I'm looking forward to retirement so I can make a few of my dreams."

"I am thirty-eight and my daughter is sixteen. I started quilting five years ago with the Folly Farm Quilters," wrote *Lynda Barnes* of Northwood, New Hampshire. "My mother quilts and *Davideen*, my daughter, made a baby quilt for her brother about four years ago."

Kathy Conry was busy organizing fact sheets at The National Needlework Association and found that many people from New Hampshire wanted very much to honor Christa McAuliffe and the other astronauts from the Challenger space shuttle.

From *Susan Bickford* of Rochester came this beautiful letter. "Being a native of New Hampshire and having young children in school, my entire family was excitedly waiting for the liftoff of the space shuttle Challenger on January 28, 1986. The devastation that we all, as a nation felt, was especially difficult for those with children asking questions, which we as parents had no answer for. It was important for me to show that those astronauts' lives had made an impact on this universe and will continue to be remem-

Old Slater Mill, Pawtucket, Rhode Island

Fig. 14. Rhode Island—Kathleen Feeley and her students from Elsie's Needlecraft Center

25

bered." Her quilt square showed the seven black balloons that were released in New Hampshire and other states to represent the mourning everyone felt. The four T-38s were flying in the last comrade formation. Stars were quilted in the sky because Christa McAuliffe told us all to "reach for the stars." The names of the children they left behind were quilted on earth. She ended with, "Quilters express themselves through fabric, and I hope I have achieved expressing the nation's feelings at this time."

A group of quilters from Deerfield, New Hampshire (except one from Epping), entitled their square "Teacher in Space." Representing the group, *Mary Kelley* wrote, "We faithfully followed the colors chosen by NASA, but changed the number of stars in the sky from ten to seven to represent the lost astronauts (Figure 8). The corner square represents the state; the schoolhouse and apple for Christa McAuliffe with a quilted apple motif in the borders." All the women who took part in making the banner wrote their names in indelible ink on the back of the square. "Our group meets weekly. We sit around the kitchen table and work on our individual projects. Whenever one of us has a quilt finished and ready to go on the frame, we have an old-fashioned New England potluck luncheon and make a day of it. Everyone pitches in to get the quilt top basted and ready for quilting." She continued, "The greatest thing quilting has done for us has been a fellowship created among the group. We share our projects, ideas, troubles, and joys . . . over strips of cloth with needles and thread in hand."

Mary Anne Downs, leader of Girl Scout troup 420 from Newton, also sent a memory quilt dedicated to Christa McAuliffe, "because of the zest for life she gave to everyone." Most of these twelve- and thirteen-year-olds had never quilted before, but wanted to be part of this event.

The four seasons represented another strong theme from New Hampshire (Figure 9). *Janice Beeler*, president of the Country Roads Quilt Guild, said, "Making the banner and writing the background material made us all realize how fortunate we are to live in America, first of all, and especially New Hampshire where we are blessed with four distinct seasons." Their spring block shows the maple trees being tapped by the barn with its stone wall. The fall brings the colors of leaves, and *Pauline Scruton* made the miniature quilts for the clothesline. Winter brings the skiers to the mountains and, of course, there are the pine trees. "We all love to quilt with a passion and have designed more quilts in our heads than we could ever finish," she says.

Carol Doak's group of five from Windham also chose the four seasons and had a great time picking out the colors. They used an outline of their state and after much work realized that their tracing paper was turned over and they had done the state in reverse. After correcting the mistake they went on to complete their section with fond memories of a fun day. They have been quilting for a combined total of forty years!

From Northwood, New Hampshire, *Joann Bailey*, *Doris Pike*, and *Anne White* sent an all-cotton banner representing old Strawberry Bank, the Atlantic Ocean seaport now called Portsmouth, which is the only port on New Hampshire's short coastline (Figure 10). The fish represent the state's first industry, the tree is for the King's

Fig. 15. Rhode Island—Dawn Lyon Cullinan

Mast Pines, and the boats are gundalows, a craft unique to its waterways. The three quilters, all in their sixties, are part of an informal group—mothers and grandmothers who quilted make up their family heritages.

Sandra Hatch and *Ruth Swasey* from Newton centered their section with a twelve-inch block called White Mountain Star designed by *Gloria Cosgrove* (Figure 11). Their block was bordered and hand-quilted. "We like the results and look forward to seeing our banner with the others. It was fun to be involved."

Because TNNA was receiving so many requests for more details, "Banner Headlines" began to send out information about the quilt festival. Groups of participants were busy making plans to come to New York in order to view their work along with all the others and to be part of this exciting event. The Museum of American Folk Art, the originator of the festival, had organized dozens of workshops that would be offered over the four-day show. Limited spaces were filled almost immediately. Workshops included quilt-making demonstrations, Amish quilters, problem solving for quilt making, Hawaiian quilters, a wearable-art fashion show, clinics on quilt conservation, and a party for exhibitors given by *Art and Antiques Magazine*. Everyone was informed that TNNA would have a booth exhibit and hoped that any banner participants would stop by to meet the staff. "It should be fun to finally put the faces and voices together," it stated.

Kathy was still catching up on the mail when a new batch arrived. It was the sixtieth year for Homemaker's Extension and many contributors expressed pride in their chapter as well as their state. "Homemaker's is education above many other things in today's world," wrote *Ellen Pasley*, state cultural arts director from Thomasboro, Illinois. "It's important to reach out to others through Extension, Agricultural, and 4-H programs," she added. Her quilt used the state logo and the theme was Illinois Homemaker's Extension Federation. Like so many other participants, Ms. Pasley learned to quilt at her grandmother's knee. "Quilting added another dimension to my life on the farm. I have become rich in the enjoyment of helping others. I always have a quilt in my quilting frame."

The Homemaker's Extension theme was also used by District Director *Myrvelle Edwards* from Eclectic, Alabama. "We would consider it a great honor to be part of Alabama's representation on the banner," she wrote. The mother of three daughters, with nine grandchildren and one great-grandchild, Mrs. Edwards learned to quilt from her mother.

Similarly, *Emma Sylvester* from Silver Springs, Nevada, enjoys quilting and has been involved for fifteen years with the Lahontan Homemakers and Silver Springs Women's club. She made a rose quilt for the Nevada State Homemakers raffle to help the state officers and their committee go to the national convention. Emma works at the ranch house that was once a stopover station for supplies for the pony express riders and travels to work each day on the original path they took. Pride in her beautiful state was what inspired the design of her banner section.

Fig. 16. New York—Susan Lori Hurwich

Fig. 17. New York—Alice M. Bachraty

Fig. 18. New York—Manhattan Plaza Children's Center

Another Lahontan Homemakers member, *Clemmie Turner*, started quilting at the age of ten. Her grandmother and mother taught her to make bed covers in order to keep warm. Every member of her family sleeps under one of her quilts. One quilt was started by her grandmother, worked on by her mother, and completed by Clemmie and her daughter. When she's resting, this busy woman always has quiltwork in her lap.

The next quilt to arrive came from *Connie Meyer*, representing the Cranberry Quilters from South Hamilton, Massachusetts (Figure 12). This stunning red, white, and blue quilt features a mariner's compass block in the center bordered by sailboats. The four members who worked on this are Connie, *Alice Butler*, *Judy Morris*, and *Martha Brown*. To make this quilt, see page 126.

It was at this stage that I became aware of the TNNA project. One day Mary and I were meeting in her office. We were discussing an educational program for schools and senior groups. Nothing was mentioned about the banner. As I got up to leave, I noticed a folded pile of what looked like quilts in the corner of her office. I asked what they were for, since I've written many craft books and a few on quilting. She showed them to me and a few minutes later, as I stood waiting for the elevator, the idea struck me to create a book about the banner. I rushed back to TNNA's office with the idea, and from that day on I became intimately involved with the banner's progress.

"We're Over the Top!" was the "Banner Headlines" caption. "We are very excited to tell you that we have 339 sections registered for the *From Sea to Shining Sea* banner," it announced. The leading states were Kansas and Wyoming with twenty-nine entries, New York with twenty-one, New Hampshire with eighteen, and Rhode Island with eleven. Other good news involved a plan to take the banner on tour after it was on display at The Great American Quilt Festival. And so once the festival was over, the banner's life would just begin. All quilters and retail shops were encouraged to spread the word. Press releases were sent to local newspapers throughout the country, with special concentration given to daily and weekly papers in the areas where banner participants lived.

Since there were so many wonderful entries from Rhode Island, representatives for Slater Mills, a historic site, decided to celebrate this state's birthday in true star-spangled fashion. After the quilt festival was over, Slater Mills in Pawtucket would feature the New England sections. The Rhode Island quilters were invited to be there to discuss their involvement in this nationwide project.

The state capitol was magnificently created in stitches by *Deborah S. King* of Lincoln, Rhode Island (Figure 13). "I have always admired the architecture and grandeur of the building," she wrote. "This year is the 350th anniversary of the founding of Rhode Island and I have always wanted to create the capitol building in a piece of artwork." Deborah King, who is over sixty years old, graduated from the Rhode Island School of Design and taught there for twenty years. She has won numerous prizes, has had

Fig. 19. New York—Laure Kagen, Susan Posner, Abby Heller, and Sandra Lewis

her work published, does private commissions, and has an extensive collection of her own work. "Quilting and patchwork have been my passion and my life," she wrote.

Another exquisite quilt square came from *Kathleen Feeley* of Esmond. Her husband, Tim, helped enlarge the pattern. When asked how many hours were spent on her project, she answered, "Every waking hour of January and February!" And doesn't it look it! Nine of her students at Elsie's Needlecraft Center in Smithfield worked with her and they all took great pride in this project. Their theme is the Old Slater Mill (Figure 14). "I was brought up in Pawtucket and always visited Slater Museum with my mom as a child," she wrote. "It's a very beautiful setting right in the center of the city. The Mill was built in 1793 and was the first factory in America to produce cotton yarn successfully with water-powered machinery." Kathy is in her thirties and has been quilting for more than twelve years. She added, "I love to quilt, and when I'm not stitching I'm thinking about stitching."

Dawn Lyon Cullinan from Wickford, Rhode Island, picked the Newport Bridge, the twelve-meter boats racing on Narragansett Bay, and the lighthouse on Rose Island for her design (Figure 15). "What an honor it has been for me to contribute to the celebration of the Statue of Liberty, which to me symbolizes Life, Liberty, and Freedom, all of which make America, America. None of my past projects has been as rewarding or creatively fulfilling as this one." It took 250 hours to complete her entry.

The state of New York had twenty-one entries, one more beautiful than the next. A big apple was a popular design choice. One of the most interesting examples of this came from *Susan Lori Hurwich* of New York City (Figure 16). "My Big Apple was constructed from approximately seven hundred two-inch triangles of VIP and Ameritex fabrics in thirty-five different shades of red." Susan has been sewing for twenty-one of her twenty-nine years.

"Burgoyne Surrounded" is a popular quilt pattern representing the defeat of British General John Burgoyne at the battle of Saratoga, a turning point for the colonies in 1777 during the Revolutionary War (Figure 17). As a result, the French came over to the American side and the Americans went on to win their independence. This seemed like an appropriate design for *Alice M. Bachraty* of Williamsville, New York. She is a self-taught quilter with seven children and three grandchildren, and has been teaching quilting for twelve years. "I don't know why I quilt, I just love it," she said. To make this quilt, see page 130.

A delightful quilt was received from a preschool class of Manhattan Plaza Children's Center showing their handprints surrounding schoolhouse blocks (Figure 18). This was submitted by *Patricia M. Kravitz, Marlene Maher,* and *Sharon Macosko* from New York City.

There were many quilts made by schoolchildren in every state. From Eva, Alabama, *Marsha Oden* sent a quilt section showing the Tennessee River and its uses in her area. Marsha is fifteen and a Morgan County 4-H'er competing in county and district events. *La Tonya Leeth,* another member of this Alabama group, used the Guntersville Lake and recreational activities for her theme. She is an art student, plays basket-

Fig. 20. New York—Susan Goldsmith

ball, is an honor student, and received the good citizenship award in her school last year.

Ellen Sears worked with her fifth graders at Anchorage Public School in Kentucky and said, "I learned about quilting with the girls. Now I'm eager to start a quilt for my new baby." Their quilt represents the Kentucky Derby, Churchill Downs, and a wreath of roses.

Reatha Jackson of Louisville, Kentucky, is an art teacher at DuValle Middle School. She worked with four of her students, *Sandra Risse, Stephanie Mucker, Chris Combs,* and *Wayne Clark,* on their theme of the city's riverfront. They wrote that the riverfront has been historically important and valuable to the economy. "The Belle of Louisville steam paddleboat gliding on the Ohio River with the new skyline in the background seemed a perfect blend of our past and future," they added.

One of the most delightful projects came from *Deborah Talamantez* and The Calico Kiddies of Wichita, Kansas. Actually, the best part of their quilt square was the back, which had on it the handprints of the little girls, ranging in age from four to nine. Their sunbonnet girls and Indian hatchets represent early settlement in Kansas. The girls' mothers and grandmothers quilt and this heritage has been proudly passed down from one generation to the next. Deb wrote, "Special bonds develop from mother to daughter as a result of this. Quilting is truly a valuable inheritance. Our group meets every two weeks and each mom takes a turn teaching the lessons. This is a special time for the moms and their daughters."

From Big Piney High School in Wyoming came a machine- and hand-stitched quilt square made by a home economics class of boys. Their teacher, *Nancy Graham,* wrote to assure us that they are all great athletes, too. They had never quilted before, but wanted to represent their state and did so with the outline of the Grand Tetons against a blue sky.

Another quilt from "the Big Apple" state came from *Laure Kagen, Susan Posner, Abby Heller,* and *Sandra Lewis* (Figure 19). Their nine-patch section combined the techniques of patchwork and appliqué for the apple squares with outline quilting of the apple design in each white square. This is a design that you might like to make for yourself and you will find the how-to directions on page 132.

"I completed my banner square while watching 'A Tree Grows in Brooklyn' on TV," wrote *Susan Goldsmith* of Brooklyn, New York (Figure 20). "It's my all-time favorite novel and sums up what Brooklyn is all about." Her banner square shows the Brooklyn Bridge, a heart, and the trees appliquéd below.

From the Brownstone Quilter's Guild of Waldwick, New Jersey, came an entry sent in by their co-president, *Jeannette Rindge* (Figure 21). Their logo was appliquéd in the center, surrounded by a six-inch border of flying geese. The outside border was quilted with a lovely leaf vine, and the use of earth tone colors is quite attractive. This is a quilt pattern you might like to adapt, using your own state's symbol in the center. To make this quilt, see page 136.

Joan Madsen of Chester, New Jersey, used Clara Barton, organizer of the American Red Cross, for her design theme. Joan is a grandmother of three and owns The Emporium, a country store.

Fig. 21. New Jersey—Brownstone Quilter's Guild

Fig. 22. Maryland—Pat Zudel and Laura Etzler

Fig. 23. Virginia—Patricia R. Foskett

39

A nine-patch quilt was created by *Pat Zudel* and *Laura Etzler* of Olney, Maryland (Figure 22). They used a different symbol associated with the state in the center of each of the bold yellow, red, black, and white squares. Pat owns the Hook & Needle Boutique in Gaithersburg, where she gives quilting lessons, and Laura has a home-based handcrafts business called Laura's Loveables. To make this quilt, see page 140.

Many entries exemplified the outstanding historic events of their states. *Patricia Kelley Jones* of Powellville, Maryland, called hers, "Maryland . . . Founded on Religious Freedom," representing the original reason for this settlement in 1632. She also incorporated many religious symbols as well as the Calvert Cross, which is part of the Maryland flag.

"Maryland, My Maryland" was the theme used by the Prince George's Historical Quilt Society of Greenbelt, with the state outline appliquéd in the center and surrounded by state emblems. This group has a membership of forty and was formed to expand the knowledge and love of quilting in their county.

Ursula Schedler of Walhalla, South Carolina, used the St. Johns Lutheran Church, which was founded by Germans from Charleston in 1853. Also represented was Oconee County, which is the Gateway to the Mountains. She wrote, "I fell in love with this beautiful corner of God's earth and am glad to be able to bring it to the attention of America."

Shirley Wilson from Pine Bluff, Arkansas, is not only proud of her state, but also a true patriotic American. When she heard that there were several entries from her state, but only two from Texas, she decided to give that state a little help.

"This quilt represents the heritage of the people of Texas. *Johanna Troutman* designed the Texas Lone Star Flag just as Betsy Ross designed the flag for the United States."

Joan M. Pollock of Newington, Connecticut, wrote, "My theme is The Charter Oak. It is said that our state constitution was hidden in this tree for safekeeping and that this document served as the model for the United States Constitution." Her banner was started shortly after Christmas and fitted in between her twenty-fifth anniversary, a vacation, two sons' birthdays, her own birthday, and a bout with the flu. The last stitch was taken at eight A.M., February 21. Now that's dedication!

Everyone enjoys seeing a good example of a sampler quilt, and a real winner came in from *Patricia R. Foskett* of Verona, Virginia (Figure 23). The eight squares surrounding the center could be reproduced easily with your own state embroidered in the center. The map of Virginia was embroidered with the state flower (dogwood) and bird (cardinal), and the names of each of the eight U.S. Presidents who came from this state were embroidered under the sampler blocks. To make this quilt, see page 144.

Susie Spencer Adams from Buckingham, Virginia, is proud of her state and chose the theme Appomattox, the scene of our nation being reunited on April 9, 1865, with Lee and Grant signing the surrender. She wrote, "This square is a tribute to my paternal grandmother, who was twenty-one at the time of the Civil War's end. I was blessed to have been raised in a three-generation home . . . My grandmother made sure we knew about the Civil War and my father took us to Appomattox often. Grandmother came

Fig. 24. North Carolina—Sara Carr and Nancy Goodman

along and explained the events." This seventy-year-old woman lives alone on a six-acre farm, does all her own lawn cutting, and worked with six different clubs on this project. "My crafts have given me a full life," she added.

As you can imagine, by this time the banner was beginning to take shape and the next hurdle was to figure out a way to hang and display it once all the squares were completed. Through many phone calls, Mary Colucci located a nautical firm that could help. What was needed was a material strong enough to endure the weight of the squares, durable enough to hold up through show after show, and lightweight enough to make it easily transportable. The material came in the form of a five-inch-wide webbing used in sail making. Sure Snap, a New York–based company, wanted to add its services to this nationwide endeavor to highlight America, and so it volunteered to grommet the thousand-plus feet of webbing. Each state's section had to be detachable from the banner, and Apix Inc. of Charlotte, North Carolina, donated more than 100 feet of industrial-strength, self-gripping, hook-and-loop tape. Every state would be able to be separated and put back in place with minimal effort. The next task at hand was how to put the banner together. A lot of open space with sewing machines would be needed to handle all the material. But more quilts were arriving and everyone agreed to put this problem aside for a while. One thing at a time—and the quilts themselves were more compelling at the moment.

Two quilts came on the same day from North Carolina—one from *Sara Carr* of Charlotte, and one from *Gladys Baker* of Zebulon. Sara's quilt was designed by her friend *Nancy Goodman* with a hornet's nest and pine bough as the theme (Figure 24). The bees were chasing British soldiers and several patriots were firing on the sidelines. "We take great pride in the fact that our county declared its independence *before* July 4, 1776, on May 20," Sara wrote. The *Charlotte Observer* wrote an article about these local women and showed a picture of them holding their finished entry. It said, "The project is more than a showcase for their handiwork. It's also a way to participate in the rededication of Lady Liberty. Kathy Conry, spokeswoman for The National Needlework Association, estimates that one thousand quilters have participated."

Gladys Baker's theme, "Cape Hatteras Lighthouse," was chosen because it is an international as well as a national and state institution that stands guard over the "Graveyard of the Atlantic" off the North Carolina coast (Figure 25). She wrote, "The first structure was authorized by Congress in 1794, and the present one was completed in 1870. It is now part of the National Park system. When completed, the seawall project that is under way will surround the lighthouse and create a small island as the shoreline recedes." Gladys's first project was a pattern copied from a quilt that her mother's mother made when her mother was a little girl in the 1890s. Since then all her work has been original designs or ancestral quilt patterns and for these she has won ribbons in local shows. See page 129 for quilt design.

The Peacemakers Extension Homemaker Club of Newberry, South Carolina, created the his-

Fig. 25. North Carolina—Gladys Baker

toric Opera House of Newberry County. Its banner was quilted in an egg-and-arrowhead design to give significance to their area, which is the largest producer of eggs.

"Rainbow Row" was the theme sent by *Jill McCollum* from the East Cooper Homemakers Club of Mt. Pleasant, South Carolina, showing different colored houses that make up this national tourist attraction. And from another Homemakers Extension in Travelers Rest, Greenville County, *Edna Ivey* and *Gwen Barton* sent an outline of their state and said, "Thanks for organizing this project. We can't wait to be at the festival."

"For some reason (we won't admit what it was) the state of Georgia was appliquéd upside down once, and backwards once," wrote a group called Little Quilts from Marietta, Georgia. Fortunately, the top was pieced but not quilted, and since *Alice Berg*'s ninth-grade son discovered this she's glad he knows his geography. Log cabin quilt blocks surround the center block and create a design that other quilters might like to adapt (Figure 26). Alice, *Sylvia Johnson*, and *Mary Ellen Von Holt* are in their thirties and forties and are self-taught quilters active in quilt happenings in the Atlanta area and "love the art of quilting." To make this quilt, see page 148.

A few years ago I was teaching quilting to a group of newcomers in Florida. None of the nineteen women had ever quilted before, although several were experienced sewers. When I asked why they weren't particularly interested in quilting they said it was for two reasons. It's cold for such a short period of time that they had no need for a quilt, and most of them asso-

ciated quilts with dark colors found in cold-weather states. Perhaps this is the reason that so few entries came from this southern state. There was, however, one entry from the St. Andrew Bay Quilter's Guild in Panama City that clearly showed how proud these women are of Florida (Figure 27). All the points of interest were appliquéd on and around the state and the quilting was done by *Anna Marie Gaffney*, a seventy-five-year-old charter member of the club. All the women who worked on this project are experienced quilters. While all fifty-one members were eager and willing to participate, only a few had the time, and it was *Mary Frances Weller* who did all the designing. *Harriet West*, who helped with the appliqués, dreams of giving all six grandchildren a quilt as a graduation gift.

At TNNA, Kathy was enjoying some of the stories that came along with the quilts. The following one, which came from *Esther Thompson* of Rolette, North Dakota, was especially nice. "While making my quilt square I enjoyed many cups of coffee with my friend and neighbor *Maxine Dissette* of Wolford, who also made a square. We supported one another with ideas and suggestions. It was a lot of fun and working together on this project made us closer." This sixty-eight-year-old grandmother says she is grateful that she is able to do handwork and can drive a car to visit her children. She has lived on a farm most of her life.

Also enjoying the rural life is *Marlene Haresign* from Water Mill, New York. Her quilt square depicted "Sandy Creek Dairy County" and she planned to attend the quilt festival, traveling two days to New York City from this upstate rural community.

Fig. 26. Georgia—Little Quilts

Fig. 27. Florida—St. Andrew Bay Quilter's Guild

Fig. 28. Tennessee—Sevier County Extension Homemakers

And from *Elizabeth DiPina* of North Providence, Rhode Island: "Before leaving for a trip I stopped to read my horoscope, which said I would be before the media. My friends at Elsie's Needlecraft Shop and I had a good laugh over this as we'd hoped to get some publicity for our quilt entries. Lo and behold, while I was on the highway heading for New Jersey, the local television station called the shop to ask us to appear. The women almost called the State Police to track me down."

Several letters told stories of lifelong crafters. Two such women come from Mississippi. *Louise Adair* of Caledonia keeps a quilt on hand at all times, as does her sister. *Louise O'Reilly* from Yazoo City is state chairperson of Cultural Arts Homemakers Clubs. When she displayed her quilt to the club, she was asked to spell Mississippi. "I couldn't believe it," she said, "I had left out three letters and had to do it all over."

Verna Plackemeier of St. Charles, Missouri, represented the Northside Extension Club with an original design by *Marg Green*. Mrs. Plackemeier and her sister Lolita spent summers with two aunts who taught them to quilt. She has made well over forty quilts and each of her children, nieces, and nephews sleeps under her creations.

Using appliqué and overall quilting, *Faye H. Idol* of Sevierville, Tennessee, created a banner section on behalf of the Sevier County Extension Homemakers. It is a fine example of folk art (Figure 28).

Several other groups sent entries from Tennessee, including the Shelby County Council, whose president, Bettylu Meier, is an old hand at quilting. "It's my love, hobby, sanity!" And from *Joy* and *Edmond Anthony* of Murfreesboro

came the state flag draped over a rocking chair on their banner section called "1986 . . . Homecoming" adapted from a poster by artist M. Sloan. "This has been a whole family project with Edmond doing most of the quilting. He has been a serious quilter for four years," wrote Joy.

As anyone from Indiana knows, the Indy 500 race is a famous event (Figure 29). The Clark County Extension Homemakers knew that the color scheme would show up well on the banner, not to be missed. Representing the group, *Pat Doerstler* wrote to say that the club makes one patchwork quilt a year to raffle off for a scholarship fund. Working with Pat on this banner were *Ruth Prather* and *Juanita Weber*.

Cindi Edgerton from Wichita, Kansas, designed the Chicago skyline for her entry because she comes from Illinois (Figure 30). "I picked out my colors and when I had it all appliquéd I decided that I had it upside down. Since the design is a mirror image, this didn't cause any problem. I just flipped it over and did the quilting to show the sky and water." Having quilted for more than ten years, Cindi said she really appreciated working on this as it aroused an interest in quilting in her fifteen-year-old daughter, *Amy*. The Jayhawk banner that Amy entered represents her basketball team, and she devoted fifty hours to her project.

While many of the entries were very personal to a particular state, some of the quilters used familiar quilt patterns such as the log cabin, flying geese, variations on star patterns, as well as abstract designs. These quilts are especially appreciated because they can be duplicated, if desired, and many of them were creatively executed. One such example came from *Geri Vieaux*,

Fig. 29. Indiana—The Clark County Extension Homemakers

Mary Vogel, and *Fran Sorenson* of Rhinelander, Wisconsin (Figure 31). Their red, white, and blue colors were used to create a large star with the log cabin method. The name of their state was embroidered across the bottom. This is a good example of a quilt that anyone might like to make. *Joanna Jones* joined the group to make a second quilt, which was appliquéd with calico leaves blowing in the autumn wind (Figure 32). See pages 150 and 135 for directions on how to make both of these quilts.

The Minnesota Mavericks of Moorhead, Minnesota, sent in their quilt, which was appliquéd with Paul Bunyan and his Blue Ox (Figure 33). Those who worked on this were *Clare Johnson, Ada Fick, Susie Lang, Yvonne Rock,* and *Edde Kuehl.*

The Minnesota Quilters used the theme "Frozen State" because, wrote *Susan Stein* and *Carol Adleman* of St. Paul, "We made our banner section in February." They chose to show Lake Superior, and added, "Color, design, creativity, fellowship, and the historical aspects of quilting have made it an obsession for both of us."

Susan Kay Winkel and *Ruth Ellen Howader* of Hartford, Michigan, used the main inland lakes, the five Great Lakes, and the largest rivers as their theme. This mother-and-daughter team (Ruth's the mother) enjoy the recreational sports Lake Michigan offers. Together they've run a quilt shop for seven years and now Susan's six-year-old daughter is starting to quilt. Ruth said, "I've done needlework since the age of six. On my favorite days I quilt ten to twelve hours. In my next life I'll skip childhood and come back as a full-grown experienced quilter with needle and thimble in hand!"

Another lifelong quilter from Manton, Michigan, *Waunetteo DeRosho,* was taught by her mother at the age of four. Her quilt depicted the wolverine, her state's animal.

As the letters and quilts came pouring in at a more rapid rate, the deadline was also quickly approaching. It was becoming evident that more than time was being invested into these quilts. While all the participants truly appreciated being part of the project, some expressed their anxieties about sending their quilts off, never to see them again. You can imagine the mixed feelings of elation and sadness that occured at the moment of letting go. *Carolee Varak Knutson* of Ames, Iowa, expressed it this way: "My square traveled with me to several towns around the state. I took it everywhere, and when it was finished and time to mail it, it was hard to give it away. I probably won't see it again after putting so many hours into making it." Her quilt with the Iowa Quilter's Guild logo in the center was made with patchwork Iowa stars around it (Figure 34). This is a nice pattern to use with your logo in the center as it is an example of a traditional early quilt design. Carolee is a fifth-generation Iowa quilter. To make this quilt, see page 152.

"Pride of Iowa" was appliquéd by *Theresa Kaltenheuser* of Elkhart, Iowa (Figure 35). It was chosen as a theme because Theresa was working on an Iowa Arts Council project to improve her appliqué technique. This block came from an 1870 pattern. The yellow and black colors were used for the state bird (the goldfinch), and the white background was completely quilted. Theresa is a member of the Iowa and Des Moines area Quilters Guild. She is proud to be fifty and believes

Fig. 30. Kansas—Cindi Edgerton

that everyone has a creative side. "For me it is quilting," she wrote, "I received a ribbon for my first quilt and many since at the Iowa State Fair." See page 139 for quilt design.

As the quilts came in, notices were sent immediately to local papers. The *Des Moines Register* featured the entry from *Eillene George*, owner of the Quilt Cupboard shop in Dubuque. She designed her square in shades of cranberry, blue, and white calicoes with the center the Hawkeye block (Figure 36). It was set into the Des Moines block, which was set into the Iowa block. This square took six weeks to make.

One of the things that the fact sheets revealed is that the majority of quilters who participated have mothers, grandmothers, and daughters who are all carrying on this American tradition. Isn't it wonderful to know that all across America our children's children will someday reach into their attics only to discover an heirloom treasure, the quilts that are being made today? *Patricia* and *Elizabeth Follett* from Union, Iowa, are part of four generations of quilters, and love being members of the Iowa Quilters Guild. Their quilt, "Iowa Barns," surrounded by a border of little red barns, was designed by Elizabeth, aged fifteen.

While the quilts were coming into the office and being cataloged, local newspapers were calling to run stories on the quilters. Magazines that work months in advance wanted photographs to go with their stories about the banner. My partner and husband, Jon Aron, is a photographer and he began borrowing some of the squares to take pictures for the magazine stories.

It wasn't easy to select the best squares to use, as one was more exciting than the next. But we did manage to put together a nice collection, and from these examples we designed a layout for this book.

It wasn't so easy to convince our publisher that we had a dynamite idea here. After the festival would anyone be interested? Would we be able to continue the enthusiasm shared by a few and bring it to many in the form of a book that would cost a great deal to produce?

Fortunately my track record, the efforts of The National Needlework Association, and the continued commitment from Fineberg Publicity to keep the banner news alive were in our favor. Besides, with all the interest that the banner was generating it was obvious that The Great American Quilt Festival was just the beginning. Companies and quilting clubs as well as trade show organizers were already signing up to use the banner after the festival was over. Then it was up to Jon and me to design a book that would be both beautiful and affordable. We met with Mary Aarons, head of production at St. Martin's Press, and Barbara Anderson, our editor, to figure out the best way to do this. Unfortunately, lots and lots of color pages are costly and it would be impossible to photograph and reproduce individually all 339 squares. In the end we accepted the awesome task of choosing seventy of the best squares. Twenty-four of these would then be selected for presentation with directions for making those quilts. Because this book would be about and for quilters, it seemed appropriate to include projects that others might enjoy making. It wasn't easy to make the selections. Jon and I reviewed each of the banner

Fig. 31. Wisconsin—Geri Vieaux, Mary Vogel, and Fran Sorenson

Fig. 32. Wisconsin—Geri Vieux, Mary Vogel, Fran Sorenson, and Joanna Jones

Fig. 33. Minnesota—The Minnesota Mavericks

squares a dozen times. Our assistant, Robby Smith, who is a designer and expert quilt maker, spent three weeks evaluating each entry. When we finally had a list of ninety-five, we met with Mary Colucci and her staff at The National Needlework Association to be sure we hadn't missed one of their favorites.

Finally, we reviewed all 339 registration forms and letters that had been originally submitted. We organized them in order of states, then interesting stories, then under common interest, and finally under similar designs. We made piles of the most interesting biographies and another pile of children who had taken part. Our goal was to include something about as many people as possible and to be sure that every state was represented in some way. You can imagine how frustrating this became.

Our criteria for the twenty-four how-to projects was to select quilts that others could duplicate and designs that were somewhat generic. For example, there were so many themes where the main body of the work centered on the shape of the state. This might limit interest for making that quilt only to those who lived in the state. When these designs and execution of the quilts were exceptional, however, we included them as inspiration for others. Some of the appliquéd quilts were too personal and detailed to re-create exactly, but are included with overall directions and patterns for the general design. In this way, the quilter can add to it as he or she sees fit. The appliquéd quilt entitled "Pride of Iowa" by *Theresa Kaltenheuser,* for example, is a lovely design that anyone living in any part of the United States might like to make. And you don't have to live in Salem, Massachusetts, to choose the delightful sailboat quilt by *Connie Meyer.*

Since the quilt squares were not yet a banner, the next task at hand for TNNA was to figure out how to sew them together using the materials that had been donated for this purpose. Once again, Mary had to put on her creative thinking cap as the rest of us went back to the fun of assembling and reading fact sheets.

Quilters from Missouri produced some lovely designs and most of them learned to quilt many years ago while watching their mothers. *Arvilla Cox* is an eighty-two-year-old Joplin resident who quilted with her four sisters. Her theme was taken from her state symbols—the dogwood, bluebird, and Hawthorne tree. A similar quilt square was submitted by *Mary Davis* of Farmington, who also used the Gateway Arch and an outline of the state. *Juanita Yates* of Monroe City chose to show the Missouri Mothers Park dedicated to the state's mothers of the year. Mrs. Yates has ten children and twenty-seven grandchildren, and is president of Missouri Mothers Association. She worked on her quilt with her daughter, *Joan Benson,* and her daughter-in-law, *Nancy Yates. Dorothy Shull* of Carthage has been quilting for more than fifty years, ever since she played under her "roof quilt" while the church ladies did hand-quilting for community needs. And they still do!

There are two quilting groups called Busy Bees. One is from Winnfield, Louisiana, the other from Wetumpka, Alabama. From the first came a square made by *Carla Owen* and *Rosa Cooper.* They both have quilters in their families

Fig. 34. Iowa—Carolee Varak Knutson

and were drawn to this art form because of a love for design and color. Their quilt square design used the Louisiana state flag and seal and the state capitol building built by Huey P. Long when he was governor, symbols of Mardi Gras in New Orleans, and a scene about Winn Parish forming a free state rather than becoming part of the Confederacy.

The Alabama Busy Bees, represented by *Marilee Tankersley,* used their home, Elmore County, for their theme. Fifteen members helped quilt and appliqué historic sites. Their group meets monthly to learn to quilt and keep up to date on quilting information. They learn from each other and share patterns. Of the thirty members, some have been quilting for more than fifty years, while others are just beginning.

The Trinity Valley Quilters Guild of Ft. Worth, Texas, has 120 members, ranging in age from early twenties to mid-eighties. *Nancy Chick* wrote, "We feel very excited for our group to participate in this great event." The basic block is the Texas Quilt Square, a five-pointed star for the Lone Star State (Figure 37). They appliquéd symbols of the Longhorn steer, a cowboy hat and boots, the bluebonnet state flower, and an oil derrick.

From *Barbara Johnston* of Austin, Texas, came a quilt square that anyone might find amusing to create (Figure 38). You don't have to come from Texas to appreciate a pair of denim jeans, and Barbara's is complete with belt and loops. The back pockets were outline quilted with the state of Texas, and a red pin-dot border completes the square. This quilter is a nationally known designer and needlework instructor who had her own needlearts television series.

Anita Murphy from Kountze, Texas, worked for sixty-five hours creating her freedom of religion theme. She added the "Yellow Rose of Texas" and the famous pine trees for which East Texas is known. She wrote, "I made my first doll bed quilt when I was seven and have been quilting ever since. I have five children, and all three daughters learned to quilt at age ten. I now teach and am founder of the Golden Triangle Quilt Guild and one of nine founders of the Texas Heritage Quilt Society. We find and preserve antique quilts made by Texas women."

Since the design applications had to be submitted to TNNA for approval, many people waited expectantly to hear the news before beginning their quilts. *Helen L. Stein* of Seguin, Texas, expressed her excitement this way, "I was so shocked when you accepted my design that I called a friend and said, 'What do I do now?' She told me to make it and told another friend about it. Before I even got my head together I was getting phone calls asking to see my quilt when it was finished. So I got busy with my flag theme. I teach oil painting and every Tuesday my students would first ask how far along I was. I have to thank them all for their encouragement. Everyone is excited for me. I am the cultural arts and international understanding chairman of the Texas Extension Homemakers. We have twenty-three thousand members!" That's a lot of cheering for Helen's entry.

Lois DeMond of Chandler, Oklahoma, worked for 120 hours on her peace pipe theme, which was influenced by her state flag (Figure 39). The blue background is for the color of the flag and the border was made of Seminole patchwork.

Fig. 35. Iowa—Theresa Kaltenheuser

This border is one that any quilter might like to adapt. She wrote, "I have never worked on a project that interested so many people. When it was finished we had a party for the viewing. I will be going to New York with my son to view the banner during the festival." She went on to say that her mother took first prize at the Oklahoma State Fair and that she herself had started quilting at age five and now has a collection of fifty quilts. The *Lincoln County News* ran a story about The Great American Quilt Festival and featured Lois holding her quilt entry. The article said, "Over a dozen Oklahoma women are helping to make history literally 'come out from under the covers.'" Their governor recognized these women at a ceremony held at the state capitol and the State Arts Council sponsored a regional quilt show.

If there were to be a grand prize for the state with the most entries it would be awarded to Kansas, and perhaps to the city of Wichita, where it was almost impossible to choose the best ones. *Cathy Carroll*'s husband helped her with the design for everyone's favorite symbol of Kansas, Dorothy and the Land of Oz (Figure 40). This would make a delightful wall hanging in any child's room. Cathy worked on this for 100 hours and said, "For two weeks, if you saw me, you saw my quilt block." A member of The Prairie Quilt Guild, she is in her mid-thirties and has three sons, Eric, Matt, and Ben. See page 143 for quilt design.

While it may seem that quilting is the province of women alone, several men did participate, if only to lend moral support to their wives, daughters, and mothers. *Shirley J. Thompson* wrote, "None of the members of our West Acres Extension Homemakers Unit are artists so we asked *Denise Hembrey*'s husband, John, to help out. He came through, and as a result we had a pattern for the beautiful Indian, The Keeper of the Plains." Along with Shirley and Denise, working on the quilt were *Maxine Stelovich, Alice Morris*, and *Ann Schwarz*, all of Wichita.

Diana Gillette, also of Wichita, remembers that her dad quilted as a child and credits his influence for her current interest in quilting. Her theme was the Wichita River Festival, an annual event that takes place for ten days in May with an assortment of activities. So if you're planning a trip out that way, you might find out more about this big event.

Lois and *Melvin Larson* of Pine Bluff, Arkansas, sent in their theme "Razorback Hog" with the state outline. "My husband is retired military and I am retired civil service," she wrote. "A new craft is always a challenge. My husband contributes a lot of unique ideas and he suggested the state and flag for our quilt square. We both enjoyed working on it."

Dorothy Haines of Clearwater, Kansas, used yellow calico to depict the wheat fields indigenous to her state (Figure 41). Green pastures and the windmill, lifeline of the farm, against the blue sky give the viewer a real feeling for this area of the country.

While reading through the fact sheets from all over the country, it occurred to me that they created a wonderful travelogue. Sitting at my typewriter was like being an armchair traveler and I thought, "What a marvelous way to find out what was most significant in a state from the people who live there." If one wanted to travel on vacation to a certain part of the country it

Fig. 36. Iowa—Eillene George

Fig. 37. Texas—The Trinity Valley Quilters Guild

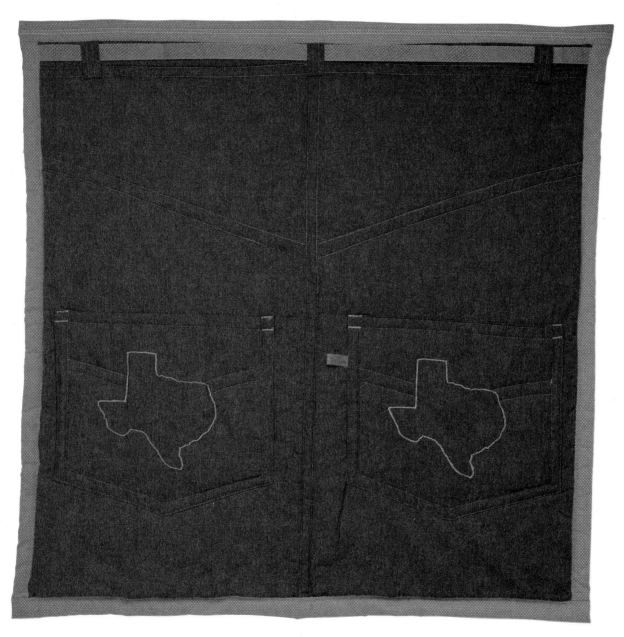

Fig. 38. Texas—Barbara Johnston

would be possible to visit a historic site described by the quilters who had stitched it into their banner section. And even if it was impossible to travel to all parts of the country, one could get a pretty, colorful overview of what's beyond one's own backyard. I've never been to Kansas, for example, but could imagine it vividly from the quilt sent by *Sigrid Simonds* representing Konza Prairie Quilt Guild of Manhattan, Kansas (Figure 42). Depicted are the Flint Hills region, stone posts cut by farmers from long ago, but still in use, the meadowlark as state bird, and the barbed wire pieced and embroidered in the border. The stone post was made from tea-dyed feed sack. Sigrid learned to quilt three years ago and *Joyce Ketterling*, who has been quilting for ten years, pieced the border. See page 147 for quilt design.

An example of excellent quilt work on an Amish theme was sent by *Sue Wettstaed* of Wichita (Figure 43). This is a quilt worth studying if you'd like to make a similar one. The directions are on page 156. She wrote, "The Amish diamond is my favorite quilt pattern. I love the dramatic color, the simplicity of design in conrast to the fancy quilting." She went on, "There is a town near Wichita called Yoder, where one sees the horse-drawn carriages and plain clothing. It makes one feel as if one has gone back to the last century." No one else in her family quilts, but Sue, who is self taught, is a charter member of the Prairie Quilt Guild. She quilts every day, which gives her a chance to be creative. "I like knowing that my work will be around when I'm gone. Quilts give people a feeling of warmth and caring and I like that too." Sue has two teenage sons, one majoring in archeology. She says that

her interest in quilting is similar to his field, and indeed it is.

Kansas residents are mighty proud of their state and a group of women from Kechi wrote to say that their theme incorporated the new state logo in celebration of Kansas's 125th birthday. *Mary Lou Roedell* and her husband, *Floyd*, own A Quilt Shoppe Etc. Their employees, *Karen Richards*, *Jan Munroe*, and *Norma McCray*, worked with them using information gathered from the Kansas Travel, Tourism and Film Services Division. Mary Lou wrote, "How appropriate. We're spreading the news on cloth from here to New York!" Floyd did all the legwork and sized the design. This seems to have been the assignment many husbands assumed. Calling all quilters' husbands! Why not start a "For Men Only" national quilters guild?

Jerri Ann Burg of Fineberg Publicity was busy placing articles in local papers all over the country, as the festival was nearing and the banner was almost complete. This created excitement from sea to shining sea. The headline in the *Wichita Eagle and Banner* declared, "Quilters Send Kansas to New York City," under which was a picture of *Anita Martz*, president of the Prairie Quilt Guild, and *Gail Hand*, surrounded by more than a dozen Kansas quilt squares. "Kansas has just gone absolutely wild," said Kathleen Conry, speaking for The National Needlework Association. The paper quoted her as saying, "Guilds in states with harsh winters generally have more quilters sewing for the banner, but none so much as the Sunflower State. I'll be honest with you," she continued, "I issued a challenge to Wyoming and told them that Kansas had so many quilt squares coming in,

Fig. 39. Oklahoma—Lois DeMond

and they could do better!''

"We happen to have a group that believes in quilting and Americana," said Anita. "They appreciate this art form." *Ruth Finnell* and *Polly Huff* quilted a portrait of Dwight D. Eisenhower. When they showed it to a relative of Mamie Eisenhower, the relative cried.

Another quilt square using Eisenhower as the theme was sent in by *Rose Mary Goetz* of Park, Kansas. She has made a quilt of all the presidents that has won several ribbons. She would love to see her square for the banner in the Eisenhower Museum at Abilene, Kansas.

Sally Brimmer and *Eleanor Malone* of Wichita, Kansas, sent their theme, "Heartland" (Figure 44). The log cabin pieced heart was appliquéd with green, yellow, and gold calicoes and solids with a border of wheat, which is grown in Kansas and milled in Missouri. Their quilt represents the Prairie Quilt Guild, the Kawvalley Quilters Guild of Lawrence, and the Quilters Guild of Greater Kansas City. Sally is in her thirties and her mother, grandmother, and two sisters quilt. She was originally inspired by her grandmother's *Kansas City Star* pattern collection. Eleanor is in her fifties and loved to watch her aunt use scraps from her mother's dresses to make quilts. Eleanor's first quilt was a single Irish chain that she made for her first grandchild. Now she has a growing interest in documenting the heritage of Kansas's quilts and quilt makers.

Beverly Sefert owns The Sewing Center in Wichita. She used the Santa Fe Trail and the Cherokee Strip for the theme of a square made with *Ann Lawson, Una Ferris, Theresa Johnson,* and *Lori McGowan.* She wrote, "I grew up as a

Mennonite and we quilted for warmth and learned to design art in fabric."

Lillie M. Webb, also from Wichita, made the "Drunkard's Path" with temperance leader Carrie Nation's hatchet (Figure 45). "The old Eaton Hotel where she broke things up still stands," she said.

Thirteen women from the Kansas group of quilters planned to go to New York to view the banner. One of them was *Nancy Hornback.* She worked on her quilt (Figure 46) with *Sandy Hysom* to appliqué a prairie woman sitting on her porch overlooking wheat fields and a solitary windmill. The woman is stitching a log cabin quilt in her lap. The name of their square is "Prairie Quilter" and it is quite lovely as you can see on page 77. Nancy has three antique rope beds in her home and wishes she had the time to cover them with her own quilts. Perhaps this project spurred her on to make quilts for her own home.

"I quilt out of respect for our pioneer women who quilted and because I enjoy it," wrote *Virginia Lamb,* representing the Walnut Valley Quilter's Guild of Arkansas City, Kansas. They chose the theme "Kansas Dugout" in honor of the pioneers who lived in home dugs into the earth (Figure 47). Brown borders represent miles of farmland, blue for the skies and orange for their sunsets, which are often that color.

Another original design came from *Jim Lane,* whose wife, Diane, wrote, "My theme, 'The Plains Indian,' was chosen because my husband is part Cherokee Indian. Wichita and Kansas are both names that are derived from the name of Indian tribes and Wichita is the home of a beautiful building called the Indian Center." The

Fig. 40. Kansas—Cathy Carroll

mother of a thirteen-year-old, *Diane Lane* is a self-taught quilter who has won numerous ribbons and awards.

Another quilt honoring Indian heritage came from *Ruth Montgomery* of Bartlesville, Oklahoma. "I feel very close to the local Indian population here," she said. "They are so proud and sharing of their culture." Her mother left some unfinished quilt tops, which launched her happily into quilting in 1970. She now teaches at five Extension Homemaker Groups, is a member of several quilters guilds, and she attends the annual Houston Quilt Festival. "Quilting for me is the most gratifying endeavor I've ever attempted," she wrote. "I especially love reaching out to new quilters." Ruth's entire family, which includes five grown sons, supports her hobby and participates in all her quilt-related projects.

Betty Shou, owner of The Fabric Hutch in Shabbona, Illinois, did an appliqué of an Indian on a horse, depicting Chief Shabbona for whom her town was named. He was instrumental in helping the early settlers and was an active peacemaker. This is a farming community and so Mrs. Shou's quilt also included crops.

While everyone at TNNA was overwhelmed by the responses from Kansas, nobody seemed to notice that Nebraskans weren't exactly doing their part. We don't mean to make an entire state feel guilty, but you should all be grateful for *Marian Heeren*, for without her efforts Nebraska would have been nonexistent on the banner lineup. From Hastings she sent her theme, "Beautiful Nebraska," from the song that she said "expresses all the wonderful things about our state that make it special." As State Cultural Arts chairperson, she felt an obligation to do her part for her state. Hooray for Marian!

Another civic-minded Cultural Arts project leader, *Luanne Jensen*, sent a quilt square representing the South Dakota Extension Homemakers Council of Marshall County. Four other members, *Esther Patterson, Ella Impecoven, Beverly Seibel*, and *Dawn Diehl*, worked with Luanne to create symbols representing the state motto. These women range in age from mid-twenties to Mrs. Patterson in her mid-seventies, who learned to quilt in her teens.

Just so Nebraskans don't feel too bad, there weren't a whole lot of entries from our Dakota states either, and one of the two groups from North Dakota actually gave a Minnesota address. However, as you can see, their entries help boost the status of the entire region in which they reside. The Old and New Quilters Club was represented by *Hilda Hinderer* of Flasher. She wrote, "Our quilt club began in 1982. Some of the members had been 'closet quilters' for years, having learned by trial and error. Other members had taken lessons from *Christy Macfield*, one of our own club members. She taught shortcut techniques, etc. We began with nine members and have grown to eighteen." They sponsor an annual quilt show and this year they will all have a sampler quilt to display. They chose a windmill to appliqué onto a blue background as the focal point of their square. The border was quilted with pieced blocks, wheat, and roses (Figure 48).

Valley Evening Quilters of Moorhead, Minnesota, created a beautiful border of a Flying Geese pattern that could be incorporated with any quilt design (Figure 49). Their choice of patterns and colors is quite attractive as well. The elevator is

Fig. 41. Kansas—Dorothy Haines

Fig. 42. Kansas—Konza Prairie Quilt Guild

Fig. 43. Kansas—Sue Wettstaed

a familiar sight in North Dakota and is the state logo. As part of the Quilters Guild of North Dakota, this project was worked on by *Yvonne Eissinger, Bette Lou Uhlman, Muriel Saign, Char Smith, Dorrie Kyllo, Mary Ellen Maltry, Edde Kuehl, Yvonne Rock, Sandy Lehrke,* and *Dorothy Smith.*

"Why would you want to do all that work?" asked *Sara Falk*'s mother and sister when she told them about the project. "I thought it would be fun. I was pregnant at the time and it was a good way to pass the time. I'm glad I did it. I even took it with me to Thanksgiving dinner," said this Tappen, North Dakota, resident who chose the buffalo for her theme.

By this time, Mary Colucci was making real progress in locating a group willing and able to sew the banner sections together. Aside from talent she needed a large enough area with many sewing machines available. This service came from the Fashion Institute of Technology in New York City. Through contact with the professors and students at the noted college of art and design, business and technology, she was guaranteed professional execution of every section and each facet of this carefully orchestrated production. The FIT students and professors were approached because of their extensive knowledge of assembly line work. They agreed to set up an assembly line to sew the grommeted webbing to the top of each individual square and a special dual needle sewing machine would be used to affix the hook and loop tape. Everything was now ready for the eventful day when the last banner section would arrive. Always one to keep things lively, Mary now set about the task of getting publicity for the "great banner sewing event."

It was still cold and damp, especially in Montana, but spring wasn't too far away when a quilt came from *Elsie Rieger,* cultural arts chairperson for the Missoula County Extension Homemaker Council. She worked with *Geneva Chaffey* and *Emma York,* who all live twenty miles apart. They passed the quilt square back and forth to complete their theme, "Indian Heritage," in recognition of the Indian cultures in Montana. Elsie started sewing and knitting at a very early age and was taught to knit by her father who learned to knit from his mother, a woman who rode West in a covered wagon. Elsie's needlework has won many blue ribbons at the Western Montana Fair. Geneva's quilts have also been blue-ribbon winners and she teaches quilting.

Another blue-ribbon winner came from Madison, Tennessee. *Freddie Kestner* quilted the square that was designed and painted by *Kay* and *John Rebello.* For their theme they chose the Parthenon, Grand Ole Opry, state flag, bird, and animal. Kay wrote, "It was with great pride that I accepted this assignment and I pray that God will bless all the ladies that worked on the banner."

Many of the quilts that came from the western states incorporated the beautiful colors found in that part of the country. They almost give the feeling of wide open spaces, and each one might be duplicated by anyone living anywhere in the United States. One of our favorites came from

Fig. 44. Kansas—Sally Brimmer and Eleanor Malone

Linda Holst of Wheatland, Wyoming (Figure 50). The Oregon Trail wound across the state, leading the way west to the promised land. The pioneer woman and covered wagon were appliquéd, silhouetted against the mountains. Linda wrote, "It is important to remember the sacrifices the pioneers made in order to follow their dreams."

Mary J. Genereux of Cheyenne, Wyoming, is a member of the Wyoming Heritage Quilt Club. This group chose the state heritage as its theme, which is depicted in four patchwork squares of brown and gold, the state colors (Figure 51). One block represents Cheyenne, another Wyoming. A third, the Teepee, is a tribute to the state's Indian population—the Shoshone and the Arapaho. The Pine Tree represents the breathtaking scenery found in Wyoming's two national parks, Yellowstone and Grand Teton. Mary owns a quilt shop where the club meets and quilts. Her dedication to quilting has brought an awareness of this artform to her city. Each block was worked on by *Deb Schultz; Pam Boley*, president; *Betty Roberts; Jan Albee*, who teaches; and *Fern Rich*, who has been piecing tops for twenty-five years. They are finishing a king-size sampler to be raffled to raise money to promote and stimulate the art of quilting in their area. To make this quilt, see page 160.

Pinedale Ward, L.D.S., Mormon Church members *Lolla Cramer* and *LuAnn Grover* of Pinedale, Wyoming, made a quilt to depict Square Top Mountain and the Green River Lakes, which are the headwaters of the Green River that flows through Utah and into the Colorado River. The quilting was done by members of the Relief Society. Eight women, ranging in age from thirty to sixty, worked together and all own quilts that they have made.

Many of the letters sent with the quilts told lovely stories about finding new friends through quilting clubs. Just as the women did in the early days of our country, today's homemakers share their talents and warmth, welcoming newcomers into the fold. One letter came from *Corinna N. Brown* of Preston, Connecticut. She is an artist who always did wall hangings and appliqué designs and started quilting them when she retired to Preston. She was asked to design a centennial quilt for thirty-five women to work. "While designing and working on that quilt, I made thirty-five friends as a newcomer to town," she said. And from *Elsie Helmer* of Moorcroft, Wyoming, "We had great fun sharing our ideas. I kept mine a secret from my family until it was done." This was her first experience with appliqué, which she wanted to use for her square. She went on, "It makes me so happy to be able to participate in this great celebration."

From the Jefferson Extension Homemakers Quilting Guild of Metairie, Louisiana, "Our guild is four years old and we have over two hundred members. We encourage beginners to join our group as we love to teach and share."

"The Great American Quilt Festival became contagious," wrote *Joan* and *Norina Hook* of Laurel, Delaware. "So we checked into hiring a bus and forty of us are coming to New York from Delaware and Maryland."

And as far away from New York as Everett, Washington, came *Diane Coombs*, vice president of Busy Bees (yes, another one, and there are more; this is a popular club name for obvious reasons).

Fig. 45. Kansas—Lillie M. Webb

Quite a few groups were making plans to come to the festival, which would be the only way they could view their work along with all the other quilt squares. After working for so many hours on a project, it was hard to send it off without wondering how it would look hanging in such a presitigious way. And who could resist seeing all the other entries? Many groups from as far away as Texas and Wyoming were making plans to be there. "Don't forget to stop by our booth to introduce yourselves," "Banner Headlines" urged. The snapshots of quilters at work or holding their squares were coming in, and each one was added to the ever-growing montage at TNNA. Its wooden plaque in the shape of the United States was filled with overlapping, smiling faces in the appropriate states. What a personal display this was creating for TNNA's booth at The Great American Quilt Festival! Mary and her staff were getting excited over the prospect of making so many new needleart friends and welcoming them into this wonderful network of shared interests.

The fellowship of quilting guilds seems to span all ages and include young women as well as great-grandmothers working side by side. This is one way for all generations to keep in touch and learn from one another. The Happy Hoopers Quilt Club of Arvada, Colorado, is one such group, whose members are also part of the Colorado Quilting Council, a statewide organization. Besides making quilts for themselves, they have made raffle quilts. The latest was "The Liberty Quilt" in red, white, and blue to raise money for the Statue of Liberty restoration fund. Before sending their section of the banner, it was hung in the State Capitol building for a few days so that the people of Colorado could view it. They wrote, "Our theme was selected because of our pride in the lofty peaks of the Rockies down to the wheat fields on the plains." As you can see by their entry (Figure 52), these women have a real feeling for color, shapes, and placement. Using calicoes and solid cottons, they have achieved their goal and given us a nice representation of their state as submitted by their chairperson, *Opal Frey.*

Another quilt that might be fun for anyone to make came from *Sally Saulmon* of Canon City, Colorado (Figure 53). She composed her block of five appliqués depicting the columbine, which is the state flower. The four pieced blocks represent an adaptation of the 1876 centennial block. Colorado became a state on the nation's hundredth birthday and is known as the Centennial State. Sally wrote, "1976 is also the year my family came to Colorado and homesteaded. I made my first quilt at age eleven. Now I try to make a full-size quilt each year and enjoy doing original design work." She has had some of her patterns published and has been teaching quilt making for several years.

Five of the eight members of the St. Vrain Valley Quilters in Longmont, Colorado, sent a representation of their gorgeous mountains and trees (Figure 54). The pieced work is an example of combining scraps of colorful textured and solid fabrics, carefully chosen and arranged. The border was outline quilted to show antelope, bighorn sheep, and the state bird, the lark bunt-

Fig. 46. Kansas—Nancy Hornback and Sandy Hysom

Fig. 47. Kansas—Walnut Valley Quilter's Guild

Fig. 48. North Dakota—The Old and New Quilters Club

ing. This group meets weekly to quilt and talk. Some are old hands, others started two years ago. Most of them have quilters in their family heritage, but have added their own styles. Their inspiration often comes from visiting exhibitions at museums and quilt shops, and from the Colorado Quilting Council, where they are members.

Quite a few groups were made up of longtime sewers and craftworkers, but many had never attempted such an ambitious quilt project. They were especially excited when their design ideas were accepted and the project took on an aura of particular specialness. From *Elizabeth Adams,* president of 2-Better-U Homemakers of Pinedale, Wyoming, came this letter. ''This is a first quilting project for our club, with most of the nineteen members being novices. We have had a lot of fun, and many of us are now interested in learning more about quilting.'' ''Green River Rendezvous'' was their chosen theme because it was a place where the trappers, mountainmen, and Indians met after a winter of hunting in order to trade and catch up on a year's happenings. The furs were used for clothing and beaver hats. The rendezvous is celebrated every year on the second Sunday in July, the main event being a historical pageant depicting the ''Meeting on the Green'' followed by a barbecue. Visiting Pinedale at this time of year should prove to be an exciting event.

Diane E. Troy from South Chatham, Massachusetts, wrote, ''I thoroughly enjoyed the time spent in the library researching the bits of Massachusetts history that I incorporated into my quilt square. I am personally related to a few historical characters and was surprised to see that persons known so well in other states were born in Massachusetts. Who knows, maybe Ben Franklin's mother was a quilter!'' This thirty-five-year-old mother of three daughters has been a quilting enthusiast for six years and said, ''I have an extremely supportive husband and family, and without them I may never have realized my quilting abilities.''

Meanwhile, more friendships were being formed as a result of this grass-roots project that was bringing people together all over the country. Can you imagine a television newscast that showed a scene with women quilting their squares in various towns at the very same moment? One such scene might show *Karen Vosen, Gail J. Searl,* and *Suzanne Huston* of Havre, Montana, working on their theme, ''Big Sky,'' with red rays of light radiating onto a royal blue background. If interviewed they would say, ''Through this quilting project some new friendships have grown. We have also been inspired to start more quilts and finished others by working together.'' Karen, who is married with one daughter age eleven, was one of twenty-nine Montana residents to needlepoint a chair seat cover for the governor's mansion and is now working on the State Seal for the National 4-H Center in Washington, D.C. Suzanne is the mother of four and an artist with a home framing business. She has a collection of antique quilts that inspired her. Her arthritis has prevented her from painting, but quilting is therapy! Gail began quilting when her first daughter was born and now all three of her daughters quilt. She is a nationally certified quilting instructor of The Embroiderer's Guild of America.

Another resident of Montana, *Shelly Van Haur*

Fig. 49. Minnesota—Valley Evening Quilters and Quilters Guild of North Dakota

of Hilger, wrote that she called her square "A Tribute to Endurance" "because my husband and I are enduring as best we can while the depression in farming continues in Montana and throughout the United States. The picture on the quilt shows a second-generation family farm with a couple in their sixties and a couple in their thirties. One sees the difference in attitudes and apparel, with the older couple showing signs of long, hard years of farming, while the younger couple looks more optimistic, and better dressed due to outside jobs to support the farm."

If you've read this far in the text, you've probably noticed that the order of contributions has not been strictly adhered to with regard to regions. As I organized the material, which was a massive job, it occurred to me that so many diversified experiences and backgrounds were also common from one part of the country to another. For example, many quilters were novices while others came from a long line of experienced needleworkers. Some people in the Northeast had similar feelings about their country as did others in the West. And many found that a famous event indigenous to their town was actually quite similar to an annual event celebrated in other parts of the country. I therefore decided to bring all these people together by intertwining their experiences to make for a richer picture of who and what this great country is made of. I hope that those whose names appear won't find it too disturbing to search for neighbors whose names might appear in another section. But perhaps in searching for those you know you will meet some new friends. Maybe

there should be a national quilting pen pal club for the purpose of creating a unique melting pot of stories and patterns for everyone to dip into. With all the quilt guilds out there, someone might just start this.

"Banner Headlines" announced the fact that I would be writing a book about the banner and everyone who participated. It said, "The stories behind the banner are one of its most intriguing features." This has certainly been proved, and while it was tempting to repeat each and every tale, editing was a big necessity or the finished book would have required a crane for lifting. Fortunately, many stories were similar and others were group efforts so that I could bring you the story behind one project made by many. As I was forced to eliminate quite a few, either because I had trouble deciphering handwriting, or because the book would be solely about Kansas (there were so many!) I kept thinking there must be enough material for another complete book.

The first group effort from Arizona was sent by *Kay Amalong*, president of the Piecemakers Guild of Tucson (Figure 55). Their quilt square is called "Cactus Flower," which is the official quilting block of Arizona. This design, with the state symbols, could be adapted for any state. Don't miss the sun and its rays quilted into the border. The state name is beautifully cross-stitched across the center block. About their state they wrote, "The forty-eighth state is truly a remarkable place, known for its breathtaking sunsets, mild winter climate, and alluring mountains. There are no words to describe the majesty and splendor of the Grand Canyon, a

Fig. 50. Wyoming—Linda Holst

Fig. 51. Wyoming—Wyoming Heritage Quilt Club

Fig. 52. Colorado—The Happy Hoopers Quilt Club

mile-deep sculptured gorge in northern Arizona.'' Fourteen tribes of Indians live within the state and a number of historical sites contain remains of early Indian cultures. Speaking for the whole group Kay said, ''It has been a joy and a privilege to be a part of *From Sea to Shining Sea.* Our guild had fun and it was nice being able to represent our state. We hope the beauty of this block reflects the pride we feel for our wonderful western state.''

An article came out in *The Salem Leader* in Salem, Indiana, telling about another proud American working on the theme ''Crossroads of America.'' *Elizabeth Marshall*, a Pekin Booster Homemaker Club member and cultural arts chairperson of Indiana Extension Homemakers, said, ''Indiana was in the direct path of the Settler's Movement to the west in the 1800s and thus the motto, 'Crossroads of America.' Hoosiers are proud to be a part of this historic event, and we are still the 'Crossroads of America.' ''

People from Arizona agree that there can be no finer sunset anywhere, and *June Rector* of Scottsdale set out to show everyone just how beautiful it can be, even in stitches (Figure 56). Many of you other quilters will surely be impressed by this exciting combination of colors, shapes, and design and might like to make a similar quilt. ''I used to watch my grandmother quilt and wanted to make a quilt for each of my four children,'' she said. *Cindy Hines* drew the design of the sun rising over the Grand Canyon for the quilt square.

Ann N. Van Ness is also from Scottsdale and her quilt square depicts an entirely different Arizona symbol, a Hopi Indian Sun Kachina head (Figure 57). ''The ancestral home of all Kachinas

is in Arizona,'' she wrote. The patchwork and quilting on this square were exquisitely executed. She ended her letter by saying, ''Quilting has become a real love. There will never be enough time to do all the quilts I've dreamed about.''

Mary A. Haddock of Alamogordo, New Mexico, used the brilliantly colored Hopi Kachina to illustrate Southwest cultures as well (Figure 58). Her interpretation came from a popular wicker basket design. It is surrounded by the Klagetoh design, commonly found in Navajo rugs. The colors are typical of her area: black, terra cotta, and turquoise. She explained, ''Alamogordo is the home of the Space Hall of Fame, White Sands National Monument, and a high-speed test track.'' She is proud to display, in her quilt, the elements that represent the Southwest. Mary belongs to the Holloman Officers' Wives Club Quilting Group and worked with *Jean Fellmeth, Jane Malcolm,* and *Marilyn Mozer.*

The natural beauty found in each state was a recurring theme across this great country of ours. *Janet Jaussaud* of Tucson used the Arizona mountains and cacti. She wrote, ''We have been so impressed with the Arizona desert, cactus, and mountains since moving here three years ago. We look out at one mountain range from the front of our house and another out the back.'' And about quilting she said, ''I love to see people express themselves through quilting.''

Margie Hockman of Bentonville, Virginia, said about her theme, ''I enjoy the beauty of the Shenandoah Valley where I live.'' Margie is a nature lover who likes to quilt as much as garden. ''I think the good Lord said, 'This person needs something to keep her sane . . . or insane

Fig. 53. Colorado—Sally Saulmon

sometimes!' So I'm addicted to quilting.''

Cathern Karlinsey of Tacoma, Washington, sent a quilt with this letter, ''Mount Rainier is the highest peak in Washington and I have a good view of it from my home.'' She also used trees, flowers, and the goldfinch, which is the state bird, in this Evergreen State. There are three generations of quilters in her family.

Like many other nature lovers, *Susanne S. Rose* of Stillwater, Oklahoma, chose the state bird (scissortail flycatcher) and flower (mistletoe) for her theme. She wrote, ''My choosing the scissortail comes from my great awe for this beautiful bird, which I have been privileged to enjoy on rare occasions, while walking.'' Sue learned to quilt the tops made by her maternal grandmother and now has a grown daughter, Pam, who shares her love of this craft.

''Branding Time'' was the title chosen by *Marylynne Lindenfeld* of Marana, Arizona, for her quilt square (Figure 59). This is a beautiful example of silhouette appliqué. Can't you just imagine being there? ''This represents my way of life,'' wrote this sixty-plus woman who still rides horses on her cattle ranch. ''The cattle industry was one of the first occupations to open up the West.'' Having quilted for more than forty years, she now teaches all phases of quilting and is especially involved with Hawaiian techniques. She is past president and historian of the Quilters Guild of Tucson. She explained her quilt in this way, ''The quilt has a double illusion. The cowboy and horse in the lower right corner can either be entering a barn and talking to the cowboy resting his horse, or he can be in the barn heading out to watch the branding. Arizona became a state in 1912 and

the symbols in the border are embroidered with registered state brands, some very old.''

Another rancher, *Bunnie Hunziker* from Laramie, Wyoming, has been an Extension Homemaker for many years. This organization has been part of Wyoming history for more than fifty years and so she used the state seal for her quilt theme.

A similar Wyoming quilt came from the members of the Willow Creek Homemakers Club of Robertson. Speaking for the group, *Anna May Henry* wrote, ''The story of our great state is all told in our Great Seal. We are a ladies club from a ranching community.''

Entertainment and leisure activities play a major part in attracting people to an area. The residents of these towns are especially proud of their state's support of cultural and recreational activities. The license plates in Utah, for example, say ''Ski Utah.'' This was the theme chosen by *Linda Jean Scott* of Roy. She wrote, ''My family enjoys skiing, and the many resorts here offer diverse winter sports within easy driving distance.'' Linda's husband is an active duty officer assigned to Hill Air Force Base, and she had her first quilting class at Mountain Home Air Force Base more than ten years ago. She wrote, ''I have given many of my needlecrafts as gifts. It is relaxing and a common bond between enthusiasts of needlework all over the world.''

Elsie Dupree of Carson City, Nevada, used the theme ''Card Tricks'' to represent gaming interests in her state. This is a traditional design that you might use to create a full bed-size quilt in the colors of your choice. Elsie used silver and blue for her state colors and added red, white, and black calicoes and solids (Figure 60). If you

Fig. 54. Colorado—St. Vrain Valley Quilters

choose to re-create this pattern, simply add another "card trick" block where Elsie has placed the appliqué of the state. She wrote, "I quilt all the time, making an average of four to six quilts a year on the sewing machine and one by hand. I use them as gifts to give to loved ones." To make this quilt, see page 164.

When it comes to giving a handmade quilt as a gift of love, *Vicky Lee Covey Clark's* grandmother of Gaithersburg, Maryland, has to take first prize. She has made a quilt for each of her twenty-two grandchildren. Vicky's theme, "I Love Maryland," was represented with a heart appliqué over her state. She also used the American Mothers' emblem and the state colors. The mother of six children ages three to fifteen, she learned to quilt "from Mom and Grandma." Could it be that the next generation of the Clark family will have six more quilters?

Katherine Hadachek of Cuba, Kansas, also chose the American Mothers, Inc., logo and believes strongly in this organization. She has been a mother of the year and a Kansas Merit Mother. As a young girl she helped her mother quilt. *Linda Rist,* owner of Creative Fabrics of Belleville, helped with the square.

Perhaps the most popular theme commemorated a specific historic event in the various states. In regard to this, these particular banner sections give us a quick overview of our country's history and an increasing appreciation for the land in which we live. Using the banner sections could be an interesting way to teach schoolchildren about the history and geography of the United States.

"Children are our future," wrote *Bonnie Harvey* of Austin, Texas. "I work in a day-care center and it is obvious to me that this project is a great way to contribute to their future." Her quilt was an outline of Texas with multicolored handprints of the children all around.

"Our school children elected the Wyoming state theme for their square," wrote *Cathy Ellis,* fourth-grade teacher at Jessup Elementary School in Cheyenne. "We try to make a quilt each year as part of the Wyoming history curriculum and incorporate a theme about our state's history such as the American Indians. Parents at Jessup School are very supportive and spend hours helping."

Linda Vickrey of Daniel, Wyoming, used the 4-H Club symbol and wrote, "I selected appliqués to represent the projects in Sublette county. I believe 4-H youth are an important part of America!" Lynda does most of her quilting in the late fall and early winter, as she is a ranch wife and has "free" time then.

Rosemary T. Shawhan of St. Marys, Ohio, incorporated Grand Lake St. Marys into her quilt theme. This is the largest man-made lake in the state. Rosemary also showed Wapakoneta, the home of Neil Armstrong, the first man on the moon. It is here that one can visit the Neil Armstrong Air and Space Museum.

Rebecca Olson of Logan, Utah, called her quilt "Wedding of the Rails" for the historic event that joined East with West. *Jane Duball* of Bridgeville, Delaware, chose the theme, "Wildlife Refuges," with the Canada goose flying over much of the state. Delaware's nickname is the "Diamond State" because it is small and has much value. This theme was created with a pieced, diamond border on a quilt from *Catherine Epperly* of Newark. *Jane Parks* of Manila, Arkansas, also

Fig. 55. Arizona—Piecemakers Guild of Tucson

Fig. 56. Arizona—June Rector and Cindy Hines

Fig. 57. Arizona—Ann N. Van Ness

chose the wildlife refuge for her theme. Big Lake was formed by an earthquake that took place in 1811–1812 and was dedicated as a national wildlife refuge by President Woodrow Wilson. Jane worked with other members of the Manila Extension Homemakers Club.

In 1985 the Municipality of Anchorage Fur Rendezvous celebrated its fiftieth year. *Mary Renfrew* of Anchorage, Alaska, made her quilt square to commemorate this event using the dog team against an Anchorage high-rise skyline. "This represents the old and the new," she explained. This seventy-year-old woman attends her local quilting guild for the inspiration and companionship found there.

The theme used by *Elsie Hanson* of Marietta, Ohio, was "First Settlement 1788," since Marietta was the first planned permanent settlement in Ohio and the Northwest Territory. She wrote, "Martin's Ferry was settled two years earlier, but did not last." When Mrs. Hanson and her sister were young girls they took first and second prizes for their sewn dresses at the Ohio State Fair.

Jean B. Lee from Anderson, Indiana, worked with *Mrs. Frederick Althaus* on her theme, "Antique Cars." Her husband's grandfather, John W. Lambert, was an early pioneer in the automotive industry and is credited with inventing the first gasoline engine "horseless carriage" in 1892. She used a sketch of an authentic 1906 Lambert for her quilt square.

From *Evelyn M. Jepson*, a native of Douglas, Wyoming, for over forty-six years, came a square representing all the wagons that passed through Wyoming. She wrote, "We were the forty-fourth state in the union, the first to have

equal rights for women. 'Equal Rights' is our state motto. I also used the symbol for the only herd of wild buffalo in the United States, which can be found in Yellowstone." She went on to say that her nephew, *Michael James,* helped with her quilt and she thought the banner was a really terrific idea. "Just wish I could be there to see all the quilts displayed together."

This was a sentiment expressed by many people living in states too far to make traveling to New York feasible. It was therefore the hope of TNNA that enough organizations around the country would eventually borrow the banner, or parts of it, for local exhibitions so that everyone who participated could, at some time, see their contribution with everyone else's. It was to be such a grand display that it would be unfortunate to miss it. Toward this end, Fineberg Publicity redoubled its efforts and got the following result. One letter came from the Agricultural Extension Service of the University of Wyoming. It said, "We would be interested in displaying the banner at our State and County Fairs. Over thirty-five hundred people would see it." More requests came from Vermont Quilting Guild of Norwich University; the Ohio State Fair Exposition Center of Columbus, Ohio; Bryant College in Smithfield, Rhode Island; Eastern States Exposition in West Springfield, Massachusetts; and the Texas State Fair in Dallas. The National Extension Homemakers Council of Blacksburg, Virginia, requested its use for its annual convention, and more letters were coming in every day.

Kathy, Lois, and the two Marys began to get organized for the final push to complete the banner. They had finally moved all the way across the country to the western states, and in came a

Fig. 58. New Mexico—Mary A. Haddock, Jean Fellmeth, Jane Mal-colm, and Marilyn Mozer

lovely example of patchwork and appliqué from *Roxy Burgard* of Salem, Oregon (Figure 61). She worked with *Phyllis Blair, Ingrid Margason,* and *Carole Meyers* to compose the pine trees, log cabins, and hearts that represent life in Oregon, admitted as a state on Valentine's Day. This is a quilt that anyone might like to make and the directions can be found on page 159.

Many of the quilts had a whimsical theme, such as the "Divine Ms. Cow" stitched by *Evie Rosen* and *Marge Wild* of Wausau, Wisconsin. Evie is the owner of The Knitting Nook and the two women were pictured working on their cow, complete with sunglasses, in the *Wausau Daily Herald.* It said, "Everyone please mooooove over. She's cool, she's in the swim, and she's heading east . . ." "She's the composite of every cow we've ever known," joked Ms. Rosen. A cow with sunglasses used to be Wisconsin's tourism symbol. *Margarete Dahlke* and *Arleen Wurman* also helped with this project.

Another whimsical beauty came from *Linda K. O'Dell* of Bakersfield, California (Figure 62). She wrote, "California is a patchwork of people, resources, and tradition. The state was divided into its natural 'patchwork of counties,' hand appliquéd, and ready to be quilted by the little pioneer woman busy at work in the lower right corner. The hands are unrolling the map." Notice in the lower left corner, the map indicating sites of the gold rush, missions, Indian tribes, and Linda's house. This quilt looks as if it was fun to construct and might be an inspiration for creating your personal state map in stitches. Linda wished that she could have flown to New York for the show, but was eight months pregnant with her third baby. Congratulations from

everyone at TNNA!

Virginia Johnson of St. Louis, Missouri, sent a quilt representing the entry of the Missouri Extension Homemakers Association, depicting an ice cream cone. This symbol was selected because the ice cream cone was first born at the 1904 World's Fair in St. Louis. The following four women worked with Virginia: *Jan Delcour, Arlene Segur, June Wesolowski,* and *Gladys Barton.*

Jacque Armstrong sent a quilt from Alamogordo, New Mexico, with this letter: "Green chili is a food staple in the Southwest. Whether someone has been raised on chili and New Mexican food, or briefly exposed to it, the memories of these precious, spicy pods can linger forever. The Pueblo Indians and early Spanish colonists prized chilies as a good preservative, natural digestive, herbal medicine, and disinfectant for wounds . . . also providing nourishment and gourmet variations to American diets." This quilt square showed a string of red chilies hanging from a porch. We learned that green chilies turn red as they dry in the ristra (a string of red chilies). I think this was one of the few quilts that used a food theme.

And another whimsical entry came from *Jeanne R. Creighton* of Los Angeles. She created a humorous adaptation of California life complete with angels, cars, and palm trees (Figure 63).

Another Southern Californian, *Kimberley E. Graf* of LaMesa, wrote, "My quilt shows the surf, sun, and fun." A native of San Diego, Kimberley has been quilting for ten years. She learned to quilt from her mother, *Janet Graf,* who owns a quilt shop, which Kimberley joined after college. Janet, who comes from Spring Valley, also entered a quilt called "California Snow-

Fig. 59. Arizona—Marylynne Lindenfeld

flake," which was all hand-stitched. Kimberley said, "I had a lot of fun creating my 'California Beach Holiday' and hope many people will enjoy exploring all the activity and life going on in it."

Not everyone thought of the carefree lifestyle for their California theme. *Lindy Stool* from Lemita created a beautiful appliquéd quilt using California poppies as her motif (Figure 64). The backround was first quilted and then the appliqués were stitched on top. If one were ambitious enough, this square could be repeated as many times as needed to make a full bed cover. See page 155 for quilt design.

On a more serious note, *Charlotte D. Brough*, who owns Charlotte's Webb in San Diego, depicted the missions, which are part of the historical foundation of California. *Juanita J. Landrum* used her town's emblem and called her quilt square "Barstow's Centennial Emblem." She owns a knitting shop, where two of her customers taught her to quilt. Her next project will be a baby quilt.

Many of the women who teach quilting classes have told me that their students are always eager to begin with a full-size quilt as a first project. Once they have completed it, however, they usually turn to baby quilts or small wall hangings after that. Perhaps in the beginning it's hard to judge how long such a project will take. Once a quilter has a feeling for the scope of a bed-size quilt, it is fun to work on a project that can be done more quickly. While most of the contributors to the *From Sea to Shining Sea* banner worked for several weeks on their squares, this proved to be the most satisfying project many had ever done. The size was man-

ageable and the complexity of design was determined by each of the individuals, since they were both designer and craftworker.

Still, many quilters wrote for extensions on their time limit. Some switched from an original plan to hand-stitch their quilt, to machine quilting or appliqué because they lacked the necessary time. *Helen F. Palmer* of Winchester, Kentucky, wrote to ay that part of the work on her quilt square was done in Florida while on vacation in order to meet the deadline. Hers was an ambitious project with an appliqué of her state and, in the center, Abraham Lincoln splitting logs at the place of his birth. Daniel Boone was also placed on the map at the Cumberland Gap and the whole quilt was surrounded with miniature log cabin blocks. Helen is president of her local Clark County Homemakers Extension Council.

Several contributors worked under unusual circumstances. *Dorothy Hecox* of Cora, Wyoming, painted her quilt during the fifty hours she was snowbound in eight feet of snow with no electric power. She was also baby-sitting for her great-grandson. She represents The Bronx Homemaker Club, the oldest Extension club in Sublette County. The members of this rural club especially enjoy the birds and flowers that they chose for their quilt square.

Devotion to this project and pride of country were strongly felt by everyone participating. This enthusiasm carried many quilters along through the holidays with Thanksgiving dinners executed between stitches, birthdays missed, anniversary celebrations canceled, bouts with the flu, even a broken arm. Yet everyone whose project design was accepted came through to

Fig. 60. Nevada—Elsie Dupree

Fig. 61. Oregon—Roxy Burgard, Phyllis Blair, Ingrid Margason, and Carole Meyers

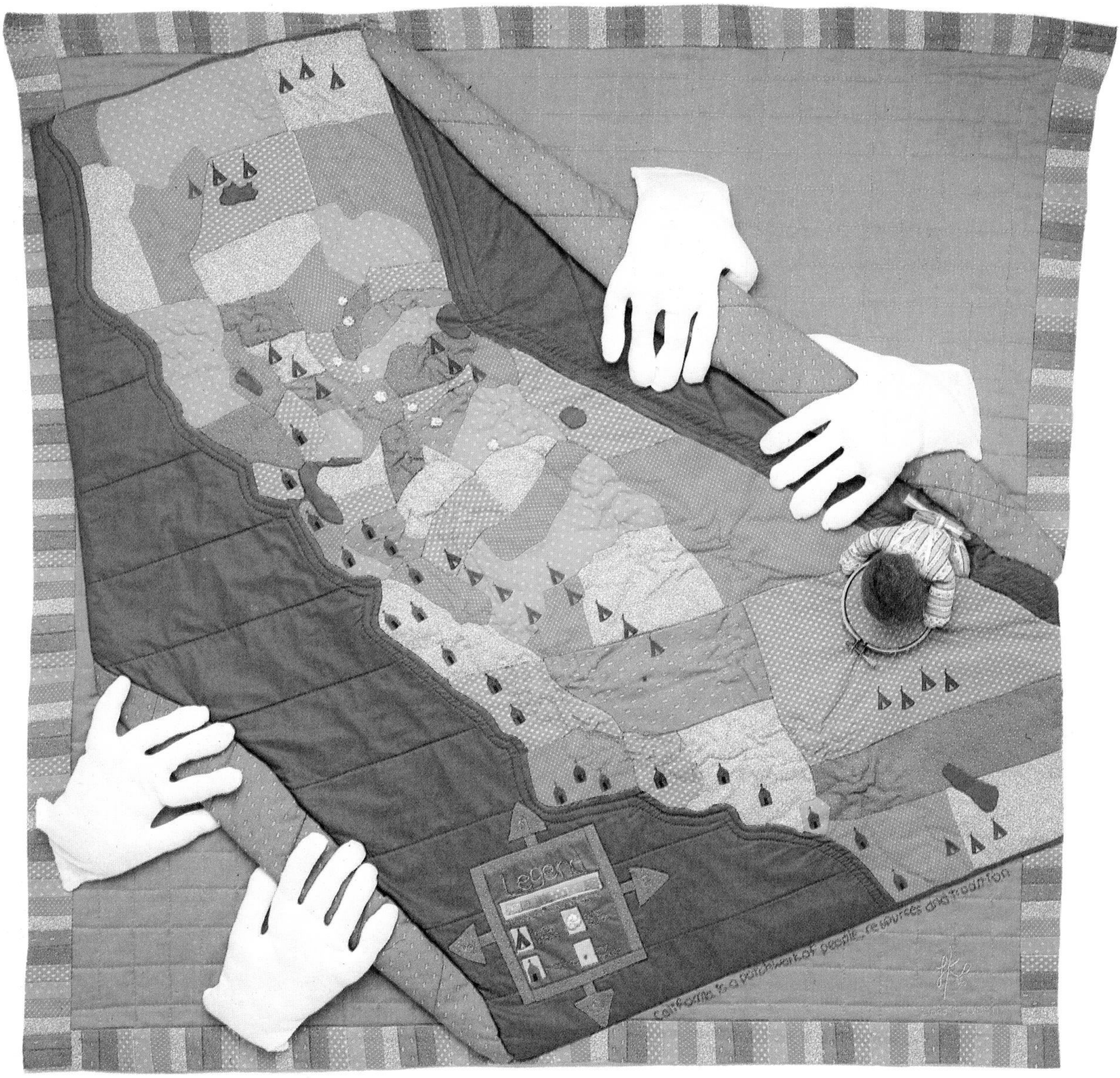

Fig. 62. California—Linda K. O'Dell

meet the deadline—or extended deadline, in some cases.

Sandra E. Long of Santa Ana, California, wrote, "When it came time to quilt my banner, my right hand was in a cast (and yes, I'm right handed!). I was not able to control the 'wrinkles' that develop during machine quilting and ended up with one on the back side of my quilt, which I named the San Andreas Fault." Her theme represents the desert, mountains, ocean, and a sunset, and she said that her kids loved all the bright colors. They want quilts for their beds just like the banner she made. As you can see from this beautiful example of patchwork, Sandy really knows how to use shades of color (Figure 65). You will find directions for making this quilt on page 168. It will be easy to adjust the design to fit any bed size. Simply extend each line of color and repeat the pattern for the length desired.

Sandy's mother, *Donna E. Friebertshauser,* of Costa Mesa, California, also made a square that was appliquéd with the state outline. She wrote, "There have been so many hours of work involved that it seems as if I've been working on it for much longer than one month. It has become a member of the family." Mrs. Friebertshauser is a needlework instructor with many years of experience in every phase of needlework.

Some of the most beautifully designed and quilted squares came from Alaska. *Beth Cassidy,* also known as *Elizabeth C. Van Devere,* of Kasilof, wrote about her quilt in this way, "The colors in my piece reflect the feel of Alaskan winters: the dull greens and browns with just a few touches of the spring colors." This quilt (Figure 66) is so serene and yet alive at the same time, which

gives us a good impression of Beth's world. She went on to say, "My husband is a commercial fisherman and it's on days like this that he first leaves for the river in mid-April. The sun just begins its long rise and we dream of long lines of salmon running beneath us." Beth is a dock foreman in the salmon industry during the summer months. She and her husband live on the Kenai peninsula where the mountains and sunsets are spectacular. This quilt was finished while Beth was on her honeymoon in the Virgin Islands and she was planning to attend the festival. Now that's traveling! But then, as she said, "I've had the passion for piecing all my life and could sew before I could read." How could she miss the greatest show on earth? To make this quilt, see page 167.

Ramona Chinn of Anchorage, Alaska, used "Land of the Midnight Sun" as her theme. Her quilt depicted the vast water with an Eskimo in a kayak surveying the seals (Figure 67).

From a tiny island that is a United States trust territory came a vibrantly colored quilt made by *Gail T. Dunn* of Tamuning, Guam (Figure 68). She wrote to say that the idea for her theme, "A Sunrise Over a Latte Stone," came from two things. Guam is known as the place where America's day begins. Thus the sunrise. "Some of the most breathtaking hues, warm colors, and shapes can be found in a Guam sunrise." The second part of Gail's inspiration came from the Latte stone. Guam was settled three thousand years ago. Pacific pioneers, known as Chamorros, fashioned large stone pillars from limestone or basalt to serve as the foundations for their homes, community houses, and canoe sheds. Throughout Guam, Latte sets mark the sites of

Fig. 63. California—Jeanne R. Creighton

Fig. 64. California—Lindy Stool

Fig. 65. California—Sandra E. Long

ancient villages. The Latte represents the strong cultural traditions of the ancestors of modern-day Guamanians.

Gail wrote, "The Statue of Liberty opens her arms to welcome visitors to the easternmost shores of America. The 'Latte of Freedom,' a proposed project of Guam's governor, will be built in order to welcome visitors from the westernmost shores of America. With this in mind it is with great pride that I submit my square to be included in the longest quilted banner ever, *From Sea to Shining Sea*."

If any of you are as curious as I was, get out your atlas. Guam is just a speck, hardly discernible in the middle of the Pacific Ocean seven hundred miles west of Hawaii. This island of more than a hundred thousand people has paved roads, a United States post office, fast food chains, and even a quilt shop. Gail owns In-Stitches and enjoys bringing needleart supplies to the people of Guam.

Janet J. Stewart of Aeia, Hawaii, wrote to say that she had a hard time parting with her square once it was finished. And no wonder! Her theme, "King Kalakaua's Crown," is a traditional Hawaiian design created for this square by Jan's "Auntie," *Debbie Kakalia*, who was scheduled to demonstrate Hawaiian quilting at the festival. Using the red and gold royal colors, it depicts the last king of the Hawaiian Islands, David Kalakaua, the first monarch to circumnavigate the earth (Figure 69). Deborah is in her forties and has been quilting for seven years. She describes herself as a "quiltaholic."

Another Hawaiian quilt came from *Susan Bushnell Nakama*, who named her creation "Where I Live There Are Rainbows." She was asked by TNNA to create the last quilt square for the banner. It depicts a rainbow stretching from Baja California, to the Hawaiian Islands (Figure 70). Susan deliberately left the rainbow unquilted so it would stand out against the heavily quilted background. This quilting design is called a "mattang," a device made of twigs with which Polynesian boys learned to navigate by studying the motion of waves deflected from islands. The border is a reproduction in cotton of a tapa cloth print. Tapa cloth is a bark cloth painted with native plant dyes and used by ancient Hawaiians for clothing, bedding, etc. She wrote, "I wanted the quilt to depict the primitive beauty in the culture and traditions of my home. Susan is in the process of making "name quilts" for her grandchildren. This is a Hawaiian custom, she explained. Last year she began the Hawaii Quilt Guild, which now has forty members. "I hope you enjoy my efforts," she wrote. "It was hard to part with it." This summed up how everyone felt about parting with their quilt squares.

Mary Colucci had arranged with a local television news station to film the sewing of the banner at The Fashion Institute of Technology. It was to be a real "happening." On the appointed day, all the sewing machines and students were ready. The lights and cameras were set up and the banner sections were sorted according to regions. Mary said, *From Sea to Shining Sea* could not have been completed without the help of so many people and the companies that contributed the materials for putting it together. It is truly an expression and reflection of

Fig. 66. Alaska—Elizabeth C. Cassidy Van Devere

Americans pulling together as one, for a single yet magnificent patriotic statement from sea to shining sea." When it was finished, Dean Jack Rittenberg of the Business and Technology department of FIT said, "Our students learn every aspect of the business and technology of fashion. The banner posed a special problem that illustrated certain complexities and gave each student an unusual and unique learning experience."

Just before the festival date, "Banner Headlines" was sent to all of the contributors. It said, "We would like to thank those who contributed and remind you to stop by to meet the TNNA staff if you are attending the festival."

Needless to say, the show was an overwhelming success. Jon and I attended early on Saturday morning and had to stand in line for an hour to get in. The crowds were shoulder to shoulder up and down every aisle, and the variety of quilts and quilt-making supplies was eye opening. But The Great American Quilt Banner captured the show, as everyone kept looking up and pointing out different states or points of interest found in each square. Seeing them all to-

gether had to be the thrill of a lifetime for those quilters who had traveled from as far away as Alaska and Hawaii, Texas, and Minnesota.

Everyone enjoyed finding her photograph on the montage of TNNA's booth, and those who didn't participate expressed wishes for another project so they could be part of it the next time. At the time of this writing, it is almost a year later and the banner is still on tour. It has been displayed, to rave reviews, at some of the largest fairs in the country. In order to photograph the quilts that appear in the book, the banner was flown from California to New York in huge crates, and then flown out to Michigan where it was booked for another appearance. The *From Sea to Shining Sea* banner has become a national celebrity that may be in demand forever. So watch your local papers for events in your area that might include the banner. Our aim is for everyone in America to view this spectacular grass-roots project that represents our nation's people in such a unique way.

Fig. 67. Alaska—Ramona Chinn

Fig. 68. Guam—Gail T. Dunn

110

Fig. 69. Hawaii—Janet J. Stewart

Fig. 70. Hawaii—Susan Bushnell Nakama

Instructions for Making Selected Quilts

Patchwork and Appliqué

The quilts that are featured in this book are made using basic patchwork and appliqué techniques. The following information will be useful as reference while making any of the projects shown here.

Quilting Terms

Appliqué: The technique of creating a design by cutting a shape from one fabric and stitching it to a contrasting fabric background.

Backing: The bottom piece of fabric, which is of the same weight as the top. This piece can be a solid or a printed fabric that matches the design on the top. Muslin is a good, inexpensive fabric often used for backing a quilted project.

Basting: Securing the top, batting, and backing together with long loose stitches before quilting. These stitches are removed after each section is quilted.

Batting: The soft lining that makes a quilted fabric puffy and gives a quilt warmth.

Block: Sometimes referred to as a square. Cut pieces of fabric are sewn together to create a design that forms a block.

Patchwork: Sewing together of fabric pieces to create an entire design. Sometimes the shapes form a geometric block. The blocks are then sewn together to make up the completed project.

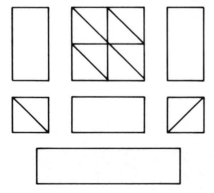
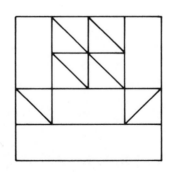

Piecing: Joining patchwork pieces together to form a design on the block.

Quilting: Stitching together 2 layers of fabric with a layer of batting between.

Quilting patterns: The lines or markings on the fabric that make up the design. Small hand or machine stitches quilt along these lines, which might be straight or curved or made up of elaborate patterns.

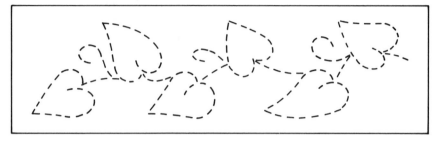

Sash or strips: The narrow pieces of fabrics used to frame the individual blocks and join them together.

Template: A pattern that is rigid and full size. It can be cut from cardboard or plastic acetate, or even sandpaper. The template is used to trace the design elements. When cutting the fabric, you will usually add ¼-inch seam allowance.

Top: The top of a quilt is the front layer of fabric with the right side showing.

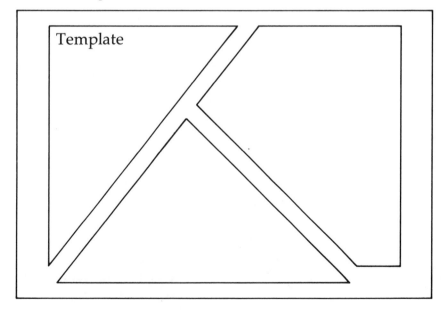

Template

Crafting How-To's

Enlarging designs and patterns: Whenever possible, designs and patterns are presented full size; occasionally, however, it is necessary to enlarge a design. In this case a grid appears over the design to be enlarged, indicating the size each square represents. Usually 1 square equals 1 inch. You then transfer the design to, or copy it onto, paper marked off into 1-inch squares. You can make your own graph paper or buy a pad in an art supply store.

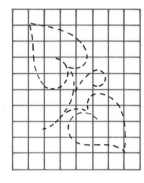 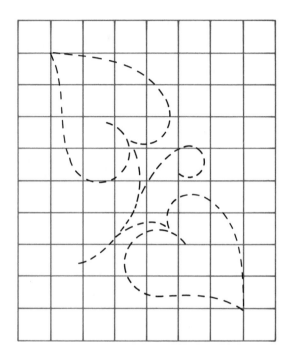

Transferring designs and patterns: Trace your design on a sheet of tracing paper, then retrace the design on the back of the tracing paper. Place the paper over the background fabric and rub a pencil over the outlines of the design. Remove the tracing and go over the design so you can see it more clearly on the fabric.

Making and using templates: To make a template, trace the outline of the design piece onto a sheet of paper. Place this face down onto thin cardboard and rub over each traced line. Go over each line with a pencil. Remove the tracing and cut out the design outline from the cardboard. Place the template on your fabric and mark around it as many times as needed. When cutting out the pieces of fabric, add ¼ inch for seam allowance.

116

How to appliqué: Using a template, cut out each pattern piece. If there is no seam allowance on your template, add ¼ inch all around when cutting. Place the template on the back of the fabric and press all edges over the template edges. If the appliqué is curved, clip all edges to seam line before turning.

Pin the appliqué in place on the background fabric and blind-stitch or whipstitch it all around. The appliquéd fabric is then backed with batting before you quilt around the design. Use short running stitches around the inside edge of the appliqué.

To machine-stitch appliqué, cut the fabric without seam allowance. Edges need not be turned. Pin the fabric in position and zigzag-stitch around the edges. When appliquéing a pointed piece, gradually narrow the zigzag width just before reaching the point on each side.

Quick and easy right triangle method: There is a quick and easy way to join light and dark triangles to create squares of any size.

Once you've determined the size of your finished unit, add 1 inch to it. For example, if you want to create 2-inch squares, you will add 1 inch. Using a yardstick, draw a grid of 3-inch squares on the lighter fabric. Next, draw diagonal lines through all squares as per diagram. With right sides facing, pin light fabric to another fabric and stitch a ¼-inch seam on each side of the drawn diagonal lines as shown.

Cut on all solid lines to get the individual units of light and dark, or contrasing fabric triangles. Clip the corners, open, and press.

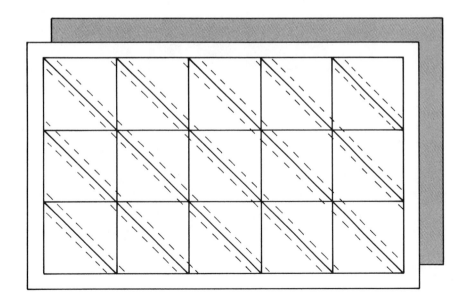

Strip piecing: This is the method by which you sew strips of different fabric together and then cut them into units that are arranged to make up the entire quilt top. Rather than cutting and sewing individual squares together over and over again, two or more strips of fabric are sewn together and then cut into segments that are of the exact same dimensions. These units are then arranged and stitched together in different positions to form the quilt pattern.

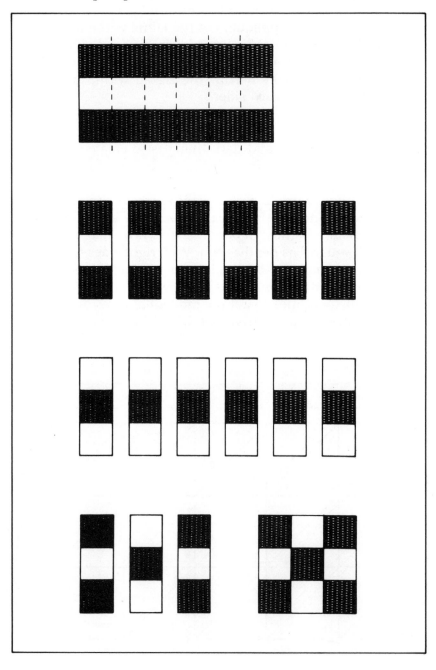

To Finish a Quilt

Preparing the backing: Begin by cutting the batting ¼ inch smaller than the quilt top all around. Next, cut a piece of backing fabric 1 inch larger than the quilt top all around. Baste the top, batting, and backing fabric together with long stitches through all three layers. Begin at the center of the quilt and baste to each outer corner. If necessary, to keep fabric from slipping, baste around outside edges as well.

Quilting: Quilting can be done on the sewing machine if you want to finish a quilt quickly. Hand-stitching makes a quilt look better, however, and adds to the charm we admire in old quilts.
1. Begin at the center of the quilt to avoid bunching of the batting and work outward, taking small running stitches ¼ inch on either side of each seam line.
2. As you approach the outer edges of the quilt, stop stitching ½ inch before reaching the quilt edge so you have not stitched in the seam line. The raw edges will be trimmed, then turned under to finish the quilt.
3. To finish a line of quilting, pull the thread through to the backing side, make a small knot, and pull back through the batting, popping the knot through the fabric. Clip the thread close to the quilt top. Or stitch over your last stitches several times to secure the end of the thread.

The last step: When all quilting is complete, clip and remove the basting stitches. Trim raw edges of backing to be even with top and fold all raw edges to the inside and press. Stitch together with a slipstitch, or blind stitch.

If you want a slight trim of the backing fabric all around the quilt top, fold the top edges under ½ inch and press. Next bring the backing fabric forward and press ¼ inch all around. Fold again over the quilt top so there is a small (¼ to ½ inch) border all around. Stitch to the front of the quilt.

Tree of Life

Maine

Materials
(45-inch-wide fabric)
small amounts assorted calicoes
small amounts brown solid
⅛ yard green calico
1½ yards white solid
½ yard navy blue solid
½ yard blue calico
1⅛ yards backing fabric
batting

Cut the following:
(includes ¼-inch seam allowance)
assorted calicoes
    39 squares 1¾ × 1¾ inches
    22 squares 2¼ × 2¼ inches—cut into 2
        triangles each
    1 square 3 × 3 inches
    4 rectangles 1¾ × 3 inches
    4 of each template piece #1, #2, and #3
    1 stem piece
brown solid
    1 each of enlarged template pieces #4, #5,
        and #6
green calico
    9 squares 3 × 3 inches—cut into 2 triangles
        each
white solid
    2 squares 19 × 19 inches—cut into 2 triangles
        each
    1 square 7 × 7 inches—cut into 2 triangles
    1 each of enlarged template pieces #7, #8,
        and #9
    1 square 3 × 3 inches
    3 squares 2½ × 2½ inches
    16 squares 3 × 3 inches—cut into 2 triangles
        each
    22 squares 2¼ × 2¼ inches—cut into 2
        triangles each
    9 squares 1¾ × 1¾ inches

navy solid—borders
    2 pieces 3 × 21½ inches
    2 pieces 3 × 36 inches
    2 pieces 1½ × 35½ inches
    2 pieces 1½ × 36½ inches
blue calico—borders
    8 pieces 1¾ × 8 inches
    8 pieces 1¾ × 10½ inches
    2 pieces 1¾ × 18½ inches
    2 pieces 1¾ × 21 inches

Fig. 1

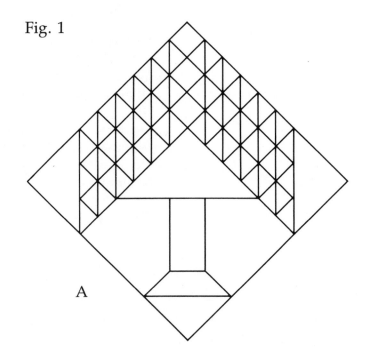

A

121

Directions
1. Join pieces to make center square (Figure 1).
2. Join blue calico border pieces to all sides.
3. Join navy blue border pieces to all sides.
4. Join a large white triangle to each side along the diagonal.
5. Join pieces to make blocks (B), (C), (D), and (E) (Figure 2).
6. Join blue calico border pieces to all 4 corner blocks.
7. Place a block in each corner. Fold all edges under and slipstitch to quilt top.
8. Join navy border pieces to quilt top.
To finish, see page 119.

Fig. 2

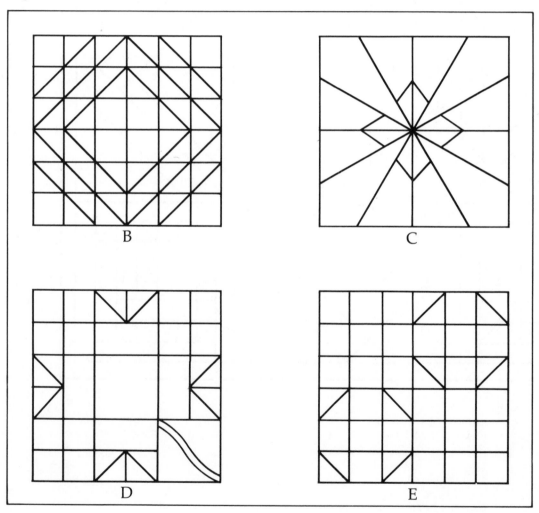

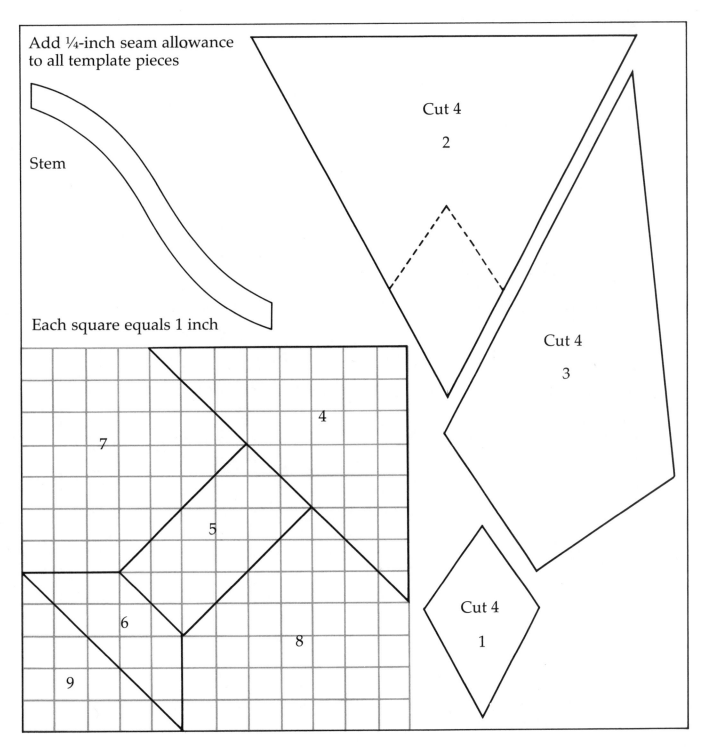

Add ¼-inch seam allowance
to all template pieces

Stem

Each square equals 1 inch

Cut 4

2

Cut 4

3

Cut 4

1

4

7

5

6

8

9

Maine

Windjammer

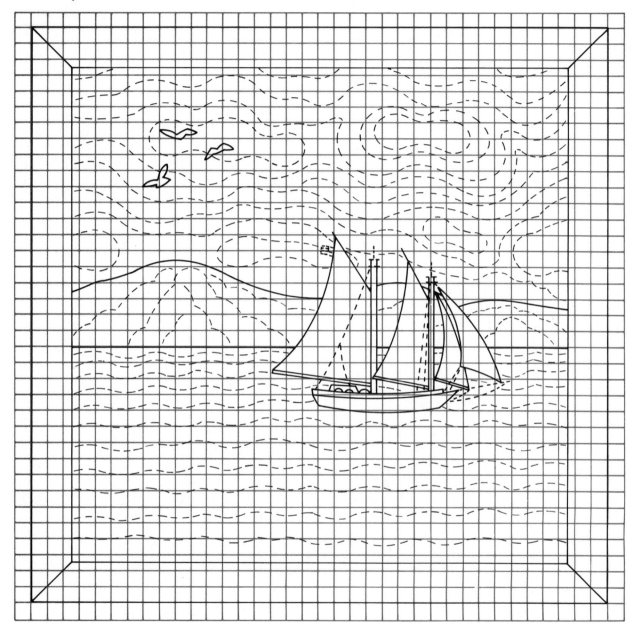

Each square equals 1 inch. To enlarge and transfer designs, see
page 116. For appliqué instructions, see page 117.

New Hampshire

Covered Bridges

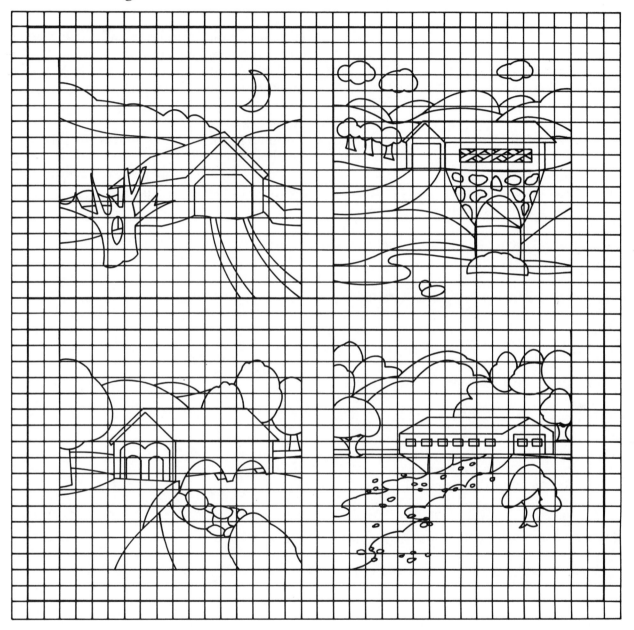

Each square equals 1 inch. To enlarge and transfer designs, see
page 116. For appliqué instructions, see page 117.

Sailboats

Massachusetts

Materials
(45-inch-wide fabric)
small piece navy blue solid (A)
¼ yard blue print (B)
½ yard red print (C)
1 yard white (D)
1⅛ yards backing fabric
batting

Cut the following:
(includes ¼-inch seam allowance)
navy blue
    4 squares 3 × 3 inches—cut into 2 triangles
      each
blue print
    34 squares 3 × 3 inches—cut into 2 triangles
      each
red print
    2 pieces 2½ × 36½ inches (border)
    2 pieces 2½ × 32½ inches (border)
    12 squares 3 × 3 inches—cut into 2 triangles
      each
    12 rectangles 2½ × 4½ inches
white
    2 pieces 2½ × 16½ inches (border)
    2 pieces 2½ × 12½ inches (border)
    12 rectangles 2½ × 8½ inches
    24 rectangles 2½ × 4½ inches
    8 squares 2½ × 2½ inches
    50 squares 3 × 3 inches—cut into 2 triangles
      each
(See "Quick and Easy Right Triangle Method,"
  page 117.)

Directions
1. Join blue print (B) triangles to white (D) triangles. Join red print (C) triangles to white (D) triangles. Join navy blue (A) triangles to white (D) triangles. (Skip this first step if you are using the "Quick and Easy Right Triangle Method.")

2. Arrange pieces in rows and stitch together to create the boat block (Figure 1). Make 12.
3. Arrange squares for center block and stitch together in rows. Then join all rows (Figure 2).
4. Join white (D) border strip to top, bottom, and sides of center block.
5. Stitch blocks together in rows as shown in the finished diagram.
6. Join rows. Join red print (C) borders to top, bottom, and sides of quilt top.
To finish, see page 119.

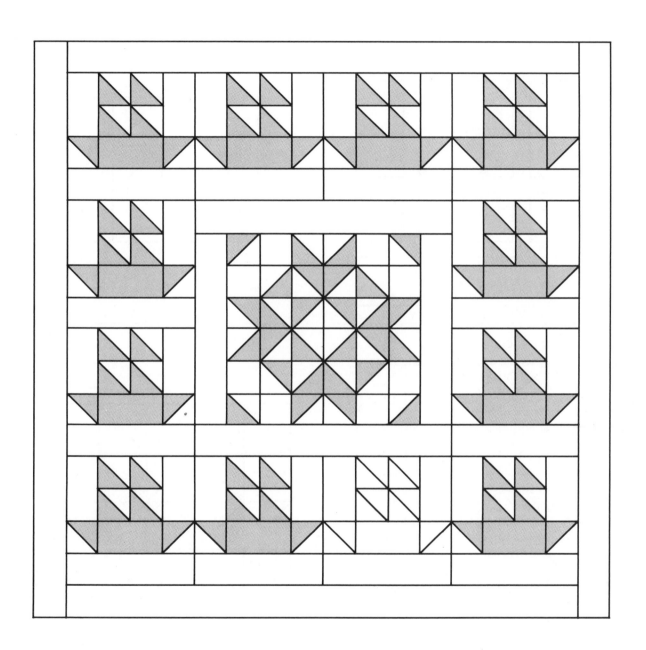

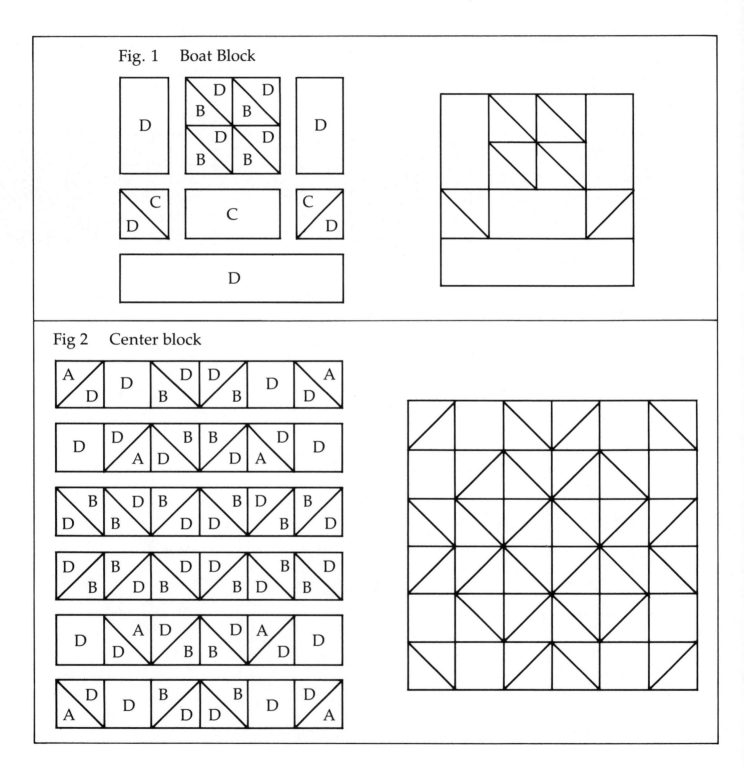

Fig. 1   Boat Block

Fig 2   Center block

North Carolina

Cape Hatteras Lighthouse

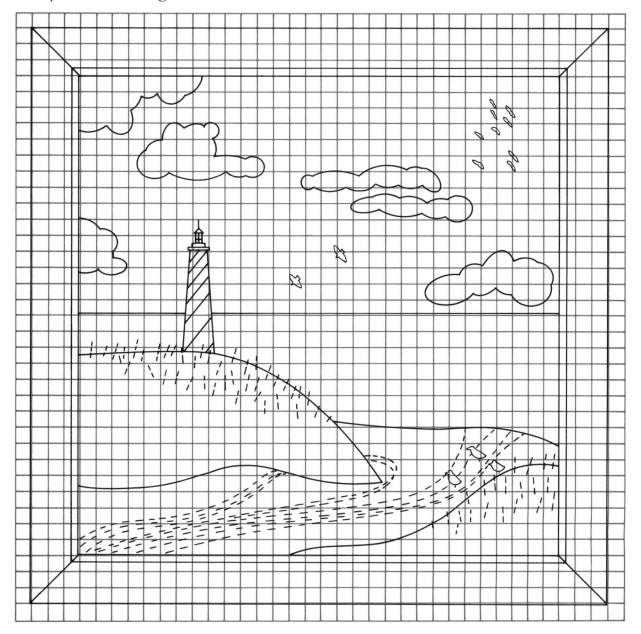

Each square equals 1 inch. To enlarge and transfer designs, see
page 116. For appliqué instructions, see page 117.

Burgoyne Surrounded

New York

Materials
(45-inch-wide fabric)
1 yard white (A)
½ yard blue (B)
½ yard red (C)
1⅛ yards backing fabric
batting

Cut the following:
(includes ¼-inch seam allowance)
white
    2 pieces 3 × 28 inches
    2 pieces 3 × 23 inches
    4 rectangles 5 × 8 inches
    8 rectangles 3½ × 5 inches
    12 rectangles 2 × 3½ inches
    28 squares 2 × 2 inches
    18 squares 3 × 3 inches—cut into 2 triangles
      each
    3 squares 3½ × 3½ inches—cut into 4
      triangles each
blue
    2 strips 2 × 33½ inches (top and bottom
      border pieces)
    2 strips 2 × 36½ inches (side border pieces)
    22 squares 3 × 3 inches—cut into 2 triangles
      each
    1 square 3½ × 3½ inches—cut into 4
      triangles
    12 squares 2 × 2 inches
    8 rectangles 2 × 3½ inches
red
    44 squares 2½ × 2½ inches
    21 squares 2 × 2 inches
    4 squares 3½ × 3½ inches

Directions
1. Join (A) and (C) squares as shown in Figure 1. Make 4.
2. Join (A), (B), and (C) squares as shown in Figure 2. Make 4.
3. Join (A), (B), and (C) pieces as shown in Figure 3. Make 4.
4. Join (A) and (C) pieces as shown in Figure 4.
5. Stitch blocks together to make rows.
6. Join all rows.
7. Add white (A) border pieces to top, bottom, and sides.
8. Stitch blue (B) and white (A) triangles to red (C) squares to form inside border (Figure 5). Join to block.
9. Add blue (B) borders to top, bottom, and sides of quilt top.
To finish, see page 119.

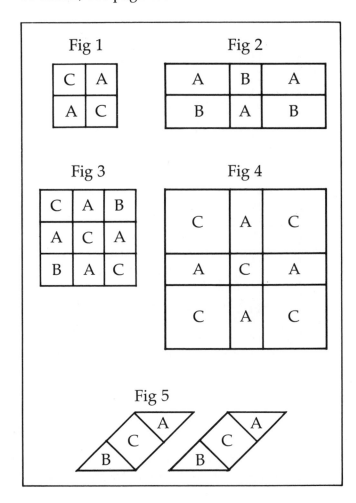

130

Apples
New York

Materials
(45-inch-wide fabric)
small amount green solid
small amount brown solid
small amount assorted red calicoes
⅛ yard of one of the red calicoes
½ yard blue calico
1⅛ yards backing
batting

Cut the following:
(includes ¼-inch seam allowance)
green
  5 pieces—leaf pattern
brown
  5 pieces—stem pattern
assorted red calicoes
  240 squares 1½ × 1½ inches
red calico
  2 pieces 1 × 35½ inches (top and bottom
    border pieces)
  2 pieces 1 × 36½ inches (side border pieces)
white
  9 squares 8½ × 8½ inches

blue calico
  2 pieces 4 × 28½ inches (top and bottom
    border pieces)
  2 pieces 4 × 35½ inches (side border pieces)
  2 strips 2½ × 28½ inches
  6 strips 2½ × 8½ inches

Directions
1. Join red squares together to make a large piece of fabric.
2. Use apple template to cut out 5 from patchwork fabric (Figure 1).
3. Appliqué apples, stems, and leaves to 5 white squares. See page 117.
4. Join blocks to make rows separated by lattice strips according to diagram. Make 3 rows.
5. Next, join rows, separated by lattice strips.
6. Join top and bottom blue border pieces. Join side border pieces.
7. Join red borders in the same way.
8. To quilt, see page 119.
To finish, see page 119.

Fig 1

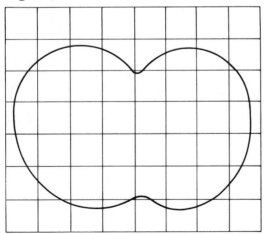

Cut apple from patchwork fabric

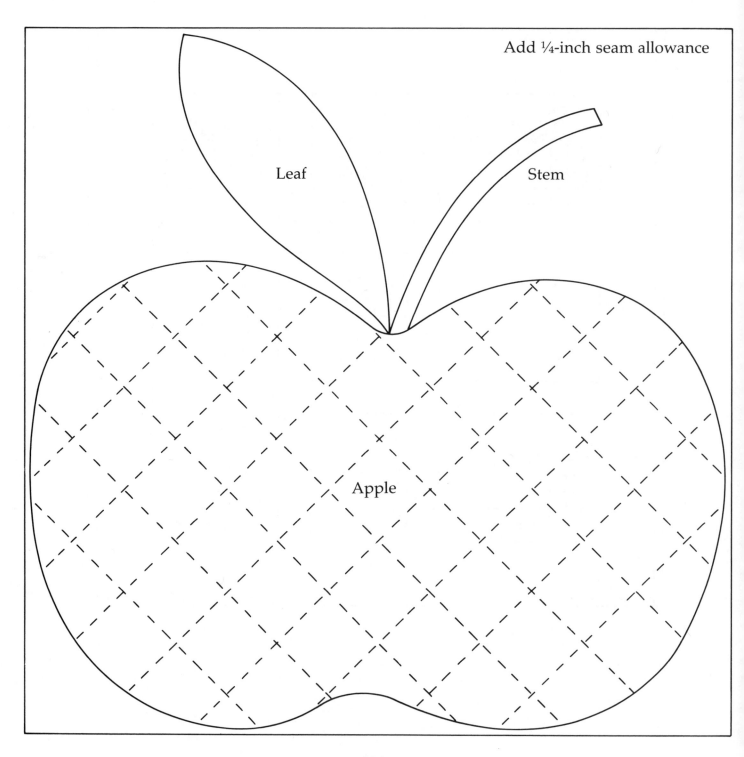

Add ¼-inch seam allowance

Leaf

Stem

Apple

Wisconsin

Autumn Leaves

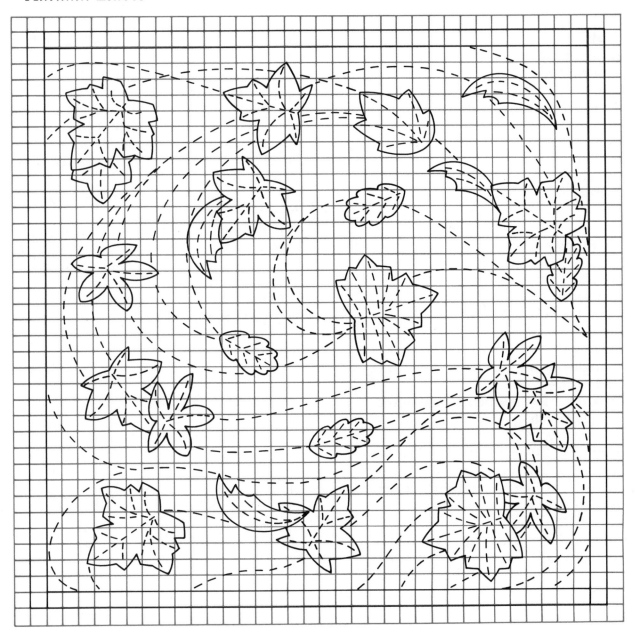

Each square equals 1 inch. To enlarge and transfer designs, see page 116. For appliqué instructions, see page 117.

Flying Geese Border
New Jersey

Materials
(45-inch-wide fabric)
small amount red calico
small amount yellow calico
small amounts assorted calicoes
⅓ yard green calico
⅓ yard tan calico
½ yard tan
⅔ yard white
1⅛ yards backing fabric
batting

Cut the following:
(includes ¼-inch seam allowance)
red calico
    2 squares 4½ × 4½ inches—cut into 4
      triangles each
yellow calico
    2 squares 4½ × 4½ inches—cut into 4
      triangles each
assorted calicoes
    24 squares 3⅛ × 3⅛ inches—cut into 2
      triangles each
green calico—borders
    2 pieces 1 × 24½ inches (top and bottom)
    2 pieces 1 × 25½ inches (sides)
    2 pieces 1½ × 34½ inches (top and bottom)
    2 pieces 1½ × 36½ inches (sides)
tan calico
    48 squares 2½ × 2½ inches—cut into 2
      triangles each
tan
    4 pieces 4½ × 25½ inches
white
    1 square 18½ × 18½ inches (center)
    4 squares 4½ × 4½ inches

Directions
1. Create an appliqué design for the center square.
2. Sew a white triangle to each short side of cal-ico triangles to make rectangles (Figure 1). Make 48.
3. Join yellow and red triangles to make 4 squares (Figure 2).
4. Join 12 patchwork rectangles along long edge. Make 3 more to create the inside borders. Attach a square at each end of each border strip. Attach to each side of center square (see diagram).
5. Join top and bottom green border pieces. Join the side border pieces.
6. Join a tan border to each side of quilt top.
7. Next, sew a white square to each short end of the remaining tan strips and attach to top and bottom of quilt.
8. Join top and bottom green border pieces. Join the side border pieces.
9. To quilt, see page 119.
To finish, see page 119.

Fig 1

Fig 2

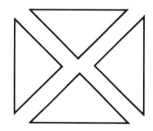
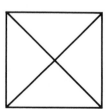

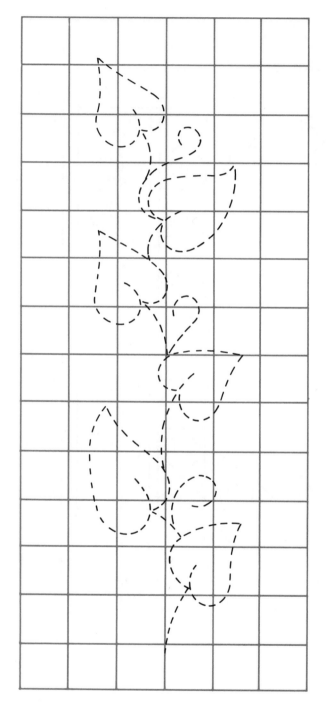

Quilting pattern

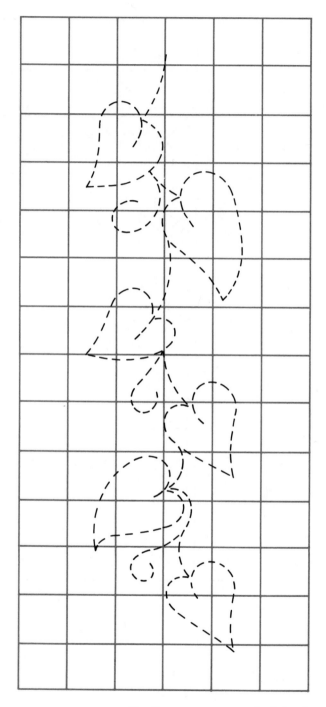

Each square equals 1 inch

138

Iowa

Pride of Iowa

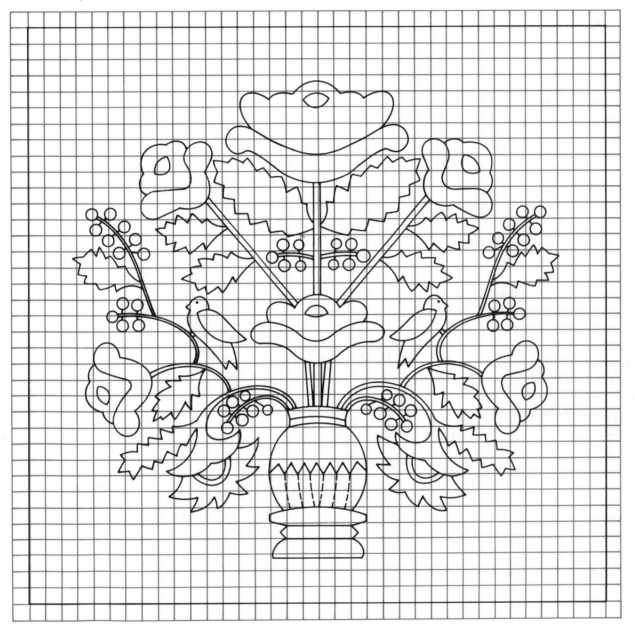

Each square equals 1 inch. To enlarge and transfer designs, see page 116. For appliqué instructions, see page 117.

Pineapple Log Cabin

Maryland

Materials
(45-inch-wide fabric)
⅓ yard white solid
½ yard yellow solid
⅔ yard red calico
⅔ yard blue calico
1⅛ yards backing fabric
batting

Cut the following:
(includes ¼-inch seam allowance)
white
   9 squares 3½ × 3½ inches
   36 pieces #8 template
yellow
   36 pieces #2 template
   36 pieces #4 template
   36 pieces #6 template
red calico
   36 pieces #3 template
   36 pieces #7 template
blue calico
   36 pieces #5 template
   2 pieces 2¾ × 32 inches (top and bottom
     border pieces)
   2 pieces 2¾ × 36½ inches (side border
     pieces)

Directions
1. Join a yellow piece #2 to each side of a white square.
2. Continue in the same way with red #3 pieces through white #8 pieces (Figure 1). Make 9 blocks.
3. Join 3 blocks to make a row. Make 3 rows.
4. Join all 3 rows.
5. Join top and bottom border pieces and then side border pieces.
To finish, see page 119.

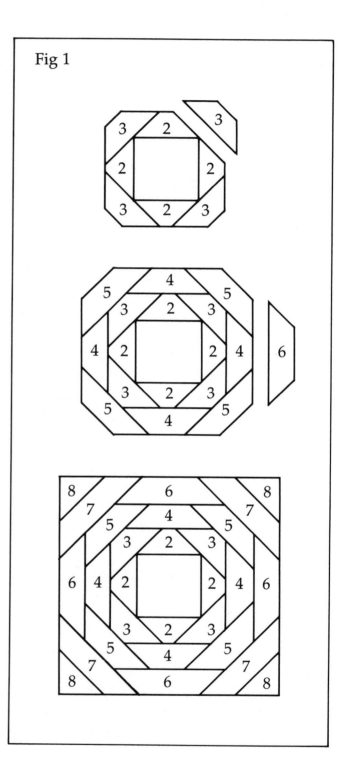

Fig 1

141

Add ¼-inch seam allowance

4

3

8

2

7

6

5

Kansas

Land of Oz

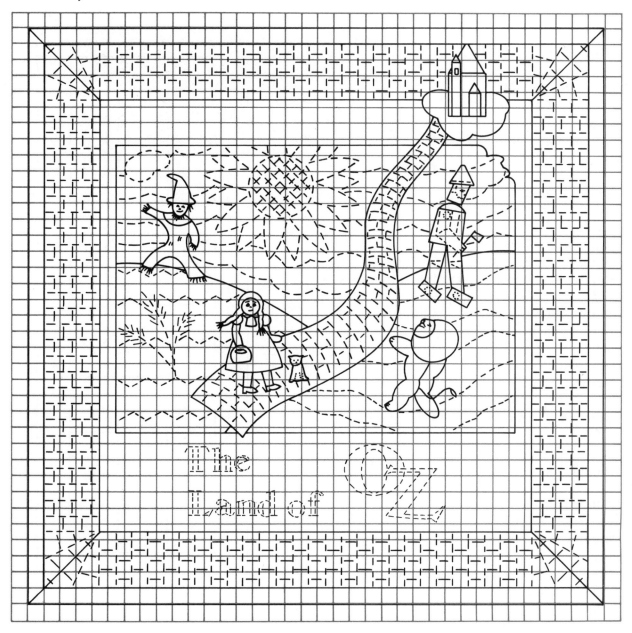

Each square equals 1 inch. To enlarge and transfer designs, see
page 116. For appliqué instructions, see page 117.

Sampler

Virginia

Materials
(45-inch-wide fabric)
⅓ yard brown calico (A)
⅓ yard beige calico (B)
½ yard white (C)
⅔ yard blue calico (D)
1¼ yards backing fabric
batting

Cut the following:
(includes ¼-inch seam allowance)
brown calico
    31 squares 2 × 2 inches
    1 square 3½ × 3½ inches
    10 squares 4 × 4 inches—cut into 2 triangles
      each
    3 squares 4½ × 4½ inches—cut into 4
      triangles each
beige calico
    16 squares 2 × 2 inches
    3 squares 3½ × 3½ inches
    4 strips 2 × 3½ inches
    5 squares 4 × 4 inches—cut into 2 triangles
      each
    2 squares 4½ × 4½ inches—cut into 4
      triangles each
white
    11 squares 3½ × 3½ inches
    20 squares 2 × 2 inches
    12 squares 4 × 4 inches—cut into 2 triangles
      each
    3 squares 2½ × 2½ inches—cut into 2
      triangles each
    4 strips 2 × 3½ inches
    1 square 9½ × 9½ inches
    4 pieces of template #1
    1 square 4½ × 4½ inches—cut into 4
      triangles each
blue calico
    6 strips 2½ × 9½ inches (lattice strips)
    2 strips 2½ × 31½ inches (lattice strips)

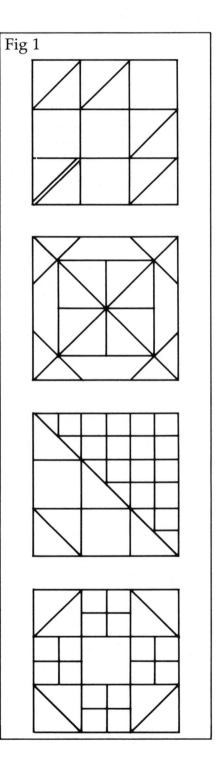

Fig 1

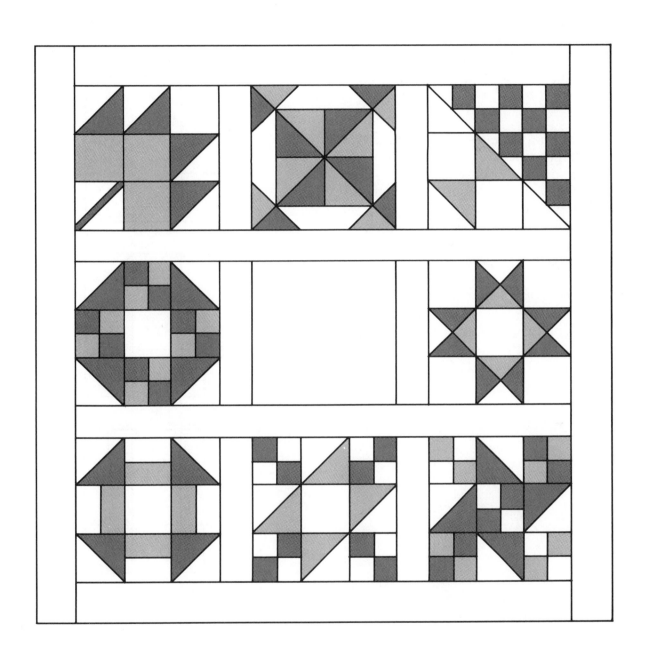

2 strips 3 × 31½ inches (top and bottom
   border pieces)
2 strips 3 × 36½ inches (side border pieces)

Directions
1. Join triangles and squares together to create
the 8 blocks (Figure 1).
2. Transfer a design representing your state
(outline the state, as an example) to the center
square and embroider.
3. Stitch 3 blocks together in a row, separated
by blue calico lattice strips. Make 3 rows.
4. Join rows together, separated by long lattice
strips.
5. Join top and bottom border pieces to quilt
top.
Join side border strips.
To finish, see page 119.

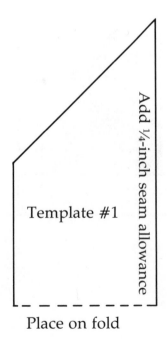

Template #1

Add ¼-inch seam allowance

Place on fold

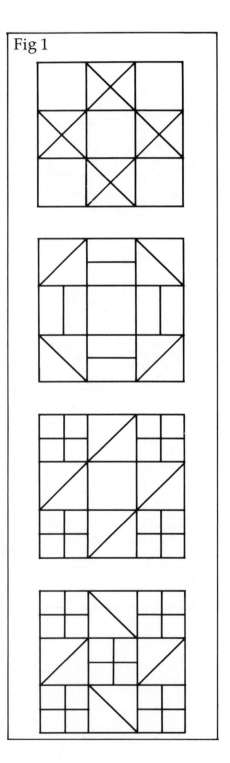

Fig 1

Kansas

Meadowlark

Each square equals 1 inch. To enlarge and transfer designs, see page 116. For appliqué instructions, see page 117.

Log Cabin Border

Georgia

Materials
(45-inch-wide fabric)
small amounts of dark calicoes
small amounts of light calicoes
¼ yard blue fabric (for borders)
⅛ yard red calico (for borders)
⅔ yard solid fabric (for center square)
small amounts of calico (center appliqué)
1¼ yards backing fabric
batting

Cut the following:
(includes ¼-inch seam allowance)
dark calicoes
    A—20 squares 1½ × 1½ inches
    C—20 pieces 1¼ × 2¼ inches
    E—20 pieces 1¼ × 3 inches
    G—20 pieces 1¼ × 3¾ inches
    I—20 pieces 1¼ × 4½ inches
    K—20 pieces 1¼ × 5¼ inches
    M—20 pieces 1¼ × 6 inches
light calicoes
    B—20 pieces 1¼ × 1½ inches
    D—20 pieces 1¼ × 2¼ inches
    F—20 pieces 1¼ × 3 inches
    H—20 pieces 1¼ × 3¾ inches
    J—20 pieces 1¼ × 4½ inches
    L—20 pieces 1¼ × 5¼ inches
blue calico borders
    2 pieces 1¼ × 21 inches (sides)
    2 pieces 1¼ × 22½ inches (top and bottom)
    2 pieces 1½ × 33½ inches (sides)
    2 pieces 1½ × 35½ inches (top and bottom)
red calico—borders
    2 pieces 1 × 35½ inches (sides)
    2 pieces 1 × 36½ inches (top and bottom)
solid
    1 square 21 × 21 inches
calico
    appliqué pieces

Directions
Appliqué
1. Design your own appliqué for the center square. You might choose your state flower or bird, or use the outline shape of your state.
2. Appliqué the design on the solid square.
3. Join brown side border pieces to the center square. Join the top and bottom border pieces to the center square.
Log Cabin Block
1. Join an A piece to a B piece.
2. Continue with a C piece. Continue joining strips to form a block (Figure 1). Make 20.
Assembly
1. Join log cabin blocks together as shown in diagram.
2. Stitch to center square to form a border of blocks.
3. Add brown side border strips. Join top and bottom strips.
4. Next, join red border strips in the same way. To finish, see page 119.

Fig 1

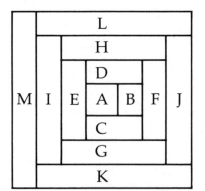

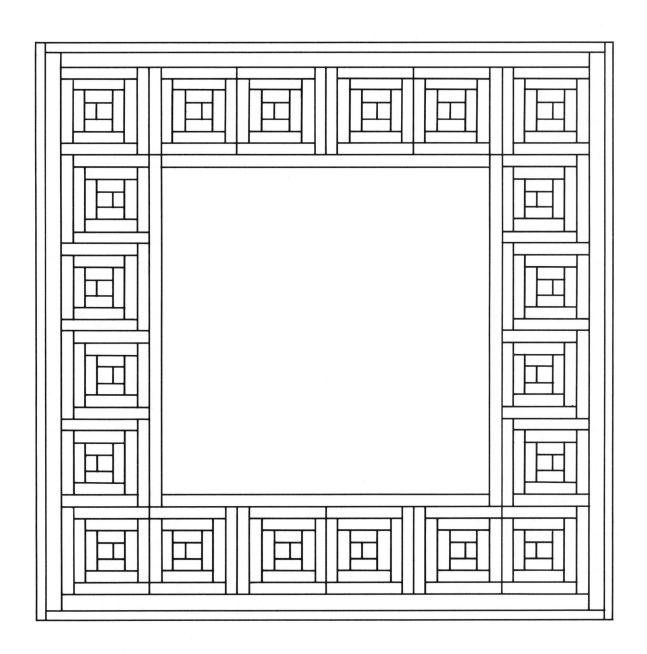

Log Cabin
Wisconsin

Materials
(45-inch-wide fabric)
⅛ yard red calico
⅛ yard orange calico
¼ yard green calico
½ yard blue calico
1 yard white
1⅛ yards backing fabric
batting

Cut the following:
(includes ¼-inch seam allowance)
red calico
    A—12 pieces 1¼ × 1¼ inches
    D—12 pieces 1¼ × 2 inches
    E—12 pieces 1¼ × 2¾ inches
orange calico
    H—12 pieces 1¼ × 3½ inches
    I—12 pieces 1¼ × 4¼ inches
green calico
    P—12 pieces 1¼ × 6½ inches
    Q—12 pieces 1¼ × 7¼ inches
blue calico
    L—12 pieces 1¼ × 5 inches
    M—12 pieces 1¼ × 5¾ inches
    2 pieces 3½ × 30½ inches (top and bottom
      border pieces)
    2 pieces 3½ × 36½ inches (side border
      pieces)
white
    A—4 pieces 1¼ × 1¼ inches
    B—20 pieces 1¼ × 1¼ inches
    C—20 pieces 1¼ × 2 inches
    D—4 pieces 1¼ × 2 inches
    E—4 pieces 1¼ × 2¾ inches
    F—20 pieces 1¼ × 2¾ inches
    G—20 pieces 1¼ × 3½ inches
    H—4 pieces 1¼ × 3½ inches
    I—4 pieces 1¼ × 4¼ inches
    J—20 pieces 1¼ × 4¼ inches
    K—20 pieces 1¼ × 5 inches

L—4 pieces 1¼ × 5 inches
M—4 pieces 1¼ × 5¾ inches
N—20 pieces 1¼ × 5¾ inches
O—20 pieces 1¼ × 6½ inches
P—4 pieces 1¼ × 6½ inches
Q—4 pieces 1¼ × 7¼ inches
2 pieces 2 × 27½ inches (top and bottom
    border pieces)
2 pieces 2 × 30½ inches (side border pieces)

Directions
1. Join an A piece to a B piece.
2. Next, join a C piece. Continue joining strips in this way to make a log cabin block (Figure 1). Make 12.
3. Make 4 blocks using all white strips (corner blocks).
4. Sew 4 blocks together to make a row. Make 4 rows.
5. Join all rows.
6. Join top and bottom white borders. Join side border pieces.
7. Join top and bottom blue border pieces. Join side pieces.

Fig 1

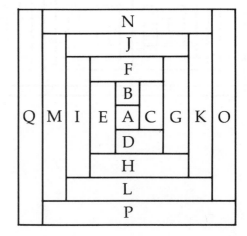

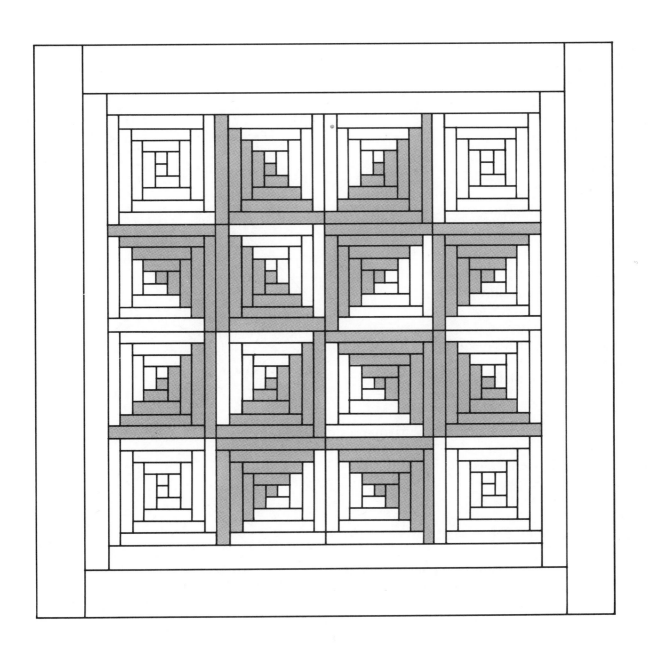

Farm Scene

Iowa

Materials
(45-inch-wide fabric)
1 yard blue calico
1 yard brown calico
small pieces floral print
scraps of rust calico
yellow calico
green calico
light blue calico
1¼ yards backing fabric
batting
tracing paper

Cut the following:
(includes ¼-inch seam allowance)
blue calico
    4 strips 2½ × 14 inches
    42 squares 4 × 4 inches—cut into 2 triangles
      each
    48 pieces from template #1
brown calico
    8 strips 2½ × 14 inches
    30 squares 4 × 4 inches—cut into 2 triangles
      each
    4 squares 2½ × 2½ inches
    16 pieces from template #1
    16 pieces from template #2
floral print
    2 squares 7¾ × 7¾ inches—cut into 2
      triangles each
Enlarge the appliqué design (see page 116) and
cut each piece from calico scraps.

Directions
1. Make the appliqué center square.
2. Join a floral triangle to each side of the appliqué square along the diagonal edge.
3. Stitch a brown strip to a blue strip and then
to another brown strip along the long edge.
Make 4.

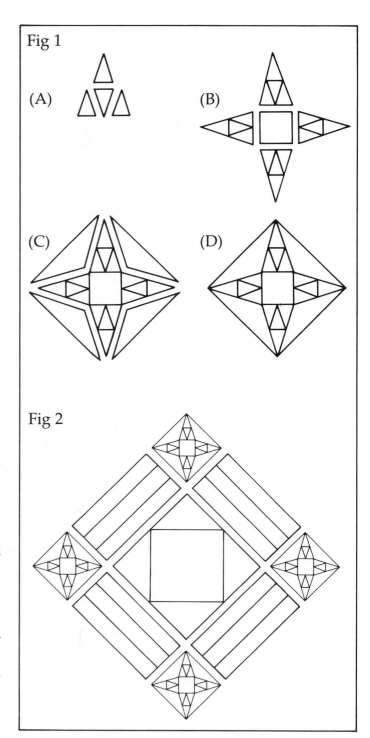

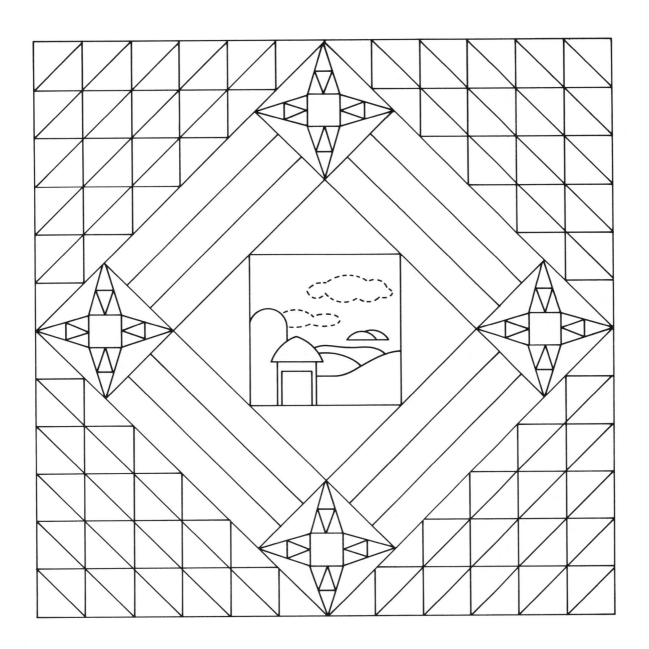

4. Stitch template pieces together to make a square as shown in Figure 1. Make 4.

5. Join squares (Figure 1) and strips to center square as shown in Figure 2.

6. Stitch brown triangles to blue triangles to make triangle corner sections of the quilt (refer to diagram). Join to each side of block.

To finish, see page 119.

Appliqué for center square

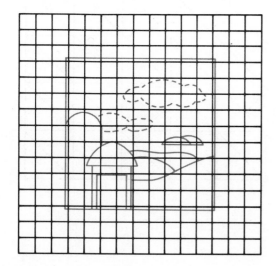

Each square equals 1 inch

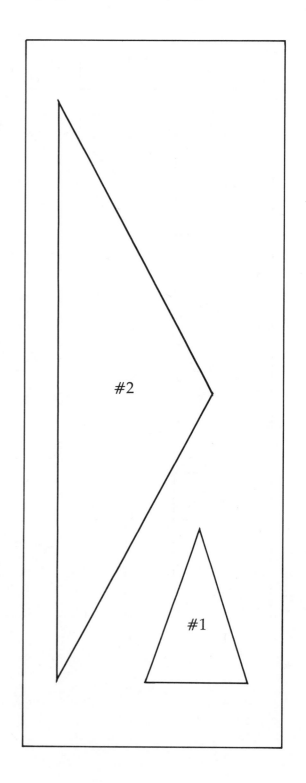

California
Poppies

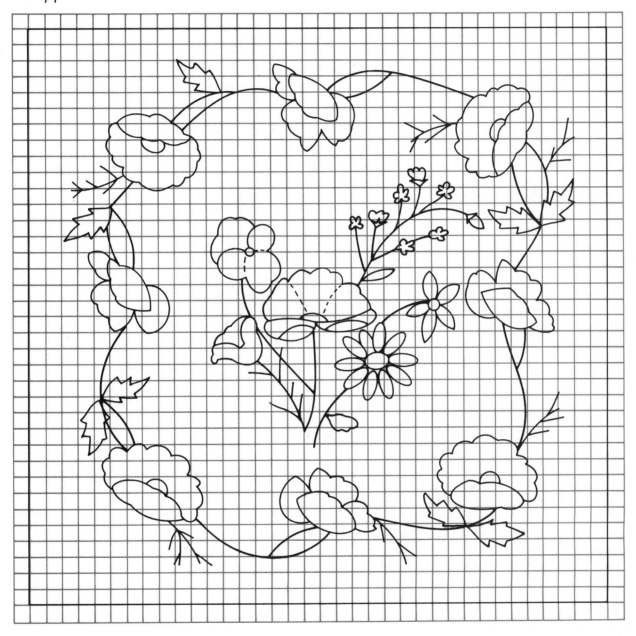

Each square equals 1 inch. To enlarge and transfer designs, see page 116. For appliqué instructions, see page 117.

Amish

Kansas

Materials
(45-inch-wide fabric)
⅛ yard black (A)
⅓ yard gray (B)
½ yard green (C)
¼ yard red (D)
1⅛ yards backing fabric
batting

Cut the following:
(includes ¼-inch seam allowance)
black
    4 pieces 2 × 14½ inches
    4 squares 2½ × 2½ inches
gray
    4 pieces 2½ × 24½ inches
    4 squares 2 × 2 inches
green
    4 pieces 4½ × 28½ inches
    2 squares 13 × 13 inches—cut into 2 triangles
        each
red
    1 square 14½ × 14½ inches
    4 squares 4½ × 4½ inches

Directions
1. Join a black (A) strip to each side of large red square.
2. Next, join a gray square to each end of the other black strips. Stitch to top and bottom of red square.
3. Join a green triangle to each side of the square along the diagonal to make a larger square.
4. Stitch a gray strip to each side.
5. Join a black square to each short end of the remaining 2 gray strips. Stitch to top and bottom edge (as you did in steps 1 and 2).
6. Join a green strip to each side edge.
7. Next, stitch a red square to each short end of remaining green strips. Join to top and bottom edge of quilt top.

Quilting
1. Baste quilt top, batting, and backing together.
2. Transfer design to top of quilt (page 116).
3. Machine or hand quilt design.
To finish, see page 119.

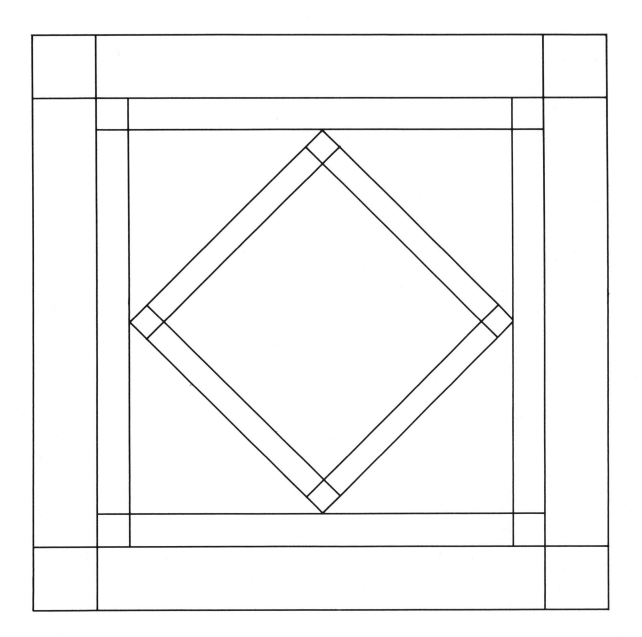

¼ of quilting pattern

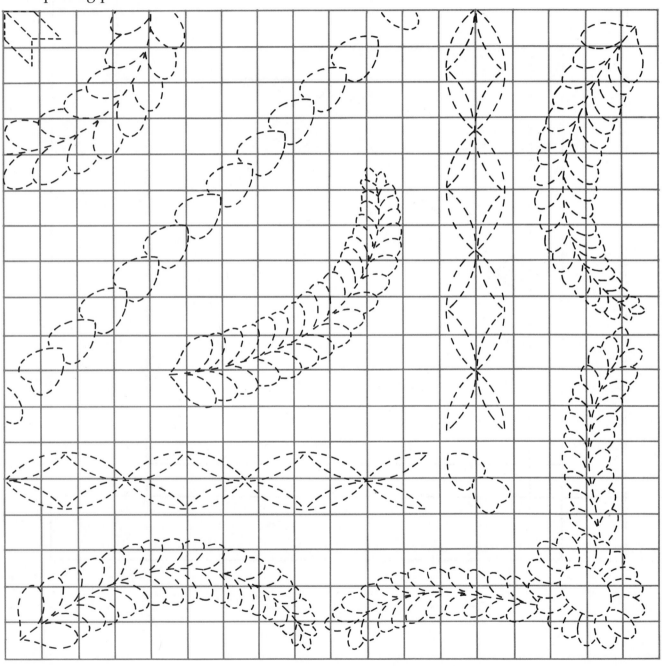

Each square equals 1 inch

Oregon

Life in Oregon

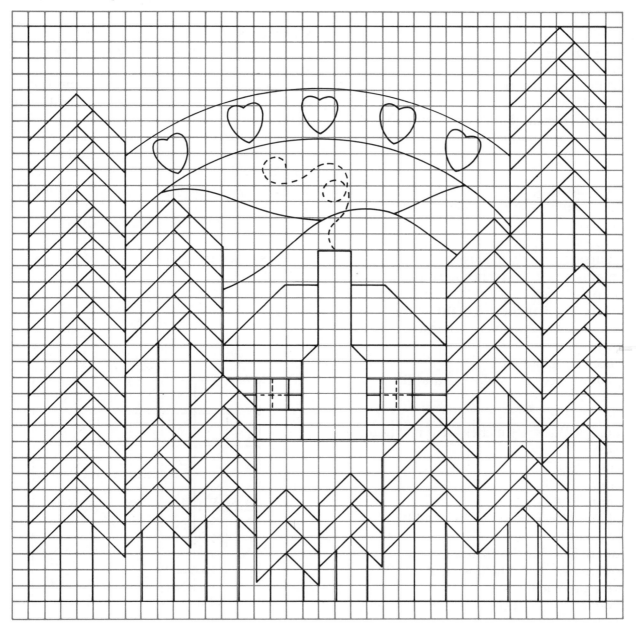

Each square equals 1 inch. To enlarge and transfer designs, see page 116. For appliqué instructions, see page 117.

Teepee Patchwork
Wyoming

Materials
(45-inch-wide fabric)
⅓ yard yellow solid (A)
½ yard brown calico (B)
½ yard yellow calico (C)
½ yard brown solid (lattice and borders)
1⅛ yards backing fabric
batting

Cut the following:
(includes ¼-inch seam allowance)
yellow solid
    4 squares 4 × 4 inches
    3 squares 2½ × 2½ inches
    2 squares 4½ × 4½ inches—cut into 2
       triangles each
    1 square 5 × 5 inches—cut into 2 triangles
    13 squares 3 × 3 inches—cut into 2 triangles
       each
    2 pieces template #1
    appliqué pieces from blocks I and III
brown calico
    4 squares 4 × 4 inches
    2 squares 4½ × 4½ inches—cut in 2 triangles
       each
    1 template #2
    1 template #3
    1 template #4
    appliqué pieces from blocks I and III
yellow calico
    1 square 5 × 5 inches (center of block IV)
    2 squares 4½ × 4½ inches—cut into 2
       triangles each
    14 squares 3 × 3 inches—cut into 2 triangles
       each
    appliqué pieces from blocks I and III
brown solid
    2 lattice strips 1½ × 14½ inches
    1 lattice strip 1½ × 29½ inches
    2 border pieces 4 × 29½ inches
    2 border pieces 4 × 36½ inches

Directions
1. Trace and enlarge appliqué pieces from blocks I and III. Cut out all pieces.
2. Appliqué blocks I and III (see page 117).
3. Join pieces to make blocks II and IV (Figure 1).
4. Join block I to block II with a lattice strip between to make top row. To make bottom row, join block II to block IV in the same way.
5. Join top row to bottom row with long lattice strip.
6. Join top and bottom border strips.
7. Join side pieces.
To finish, see page 119.

Fig 1   Block II

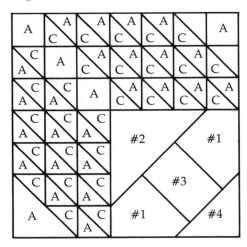

Block IV

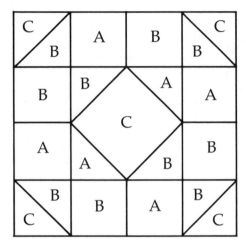

#3

cut 1

Block I

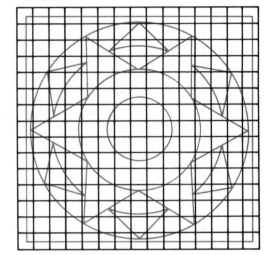

Each square equals 1 inch

Block III

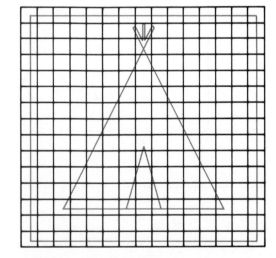

Each square equals 1 inch

162

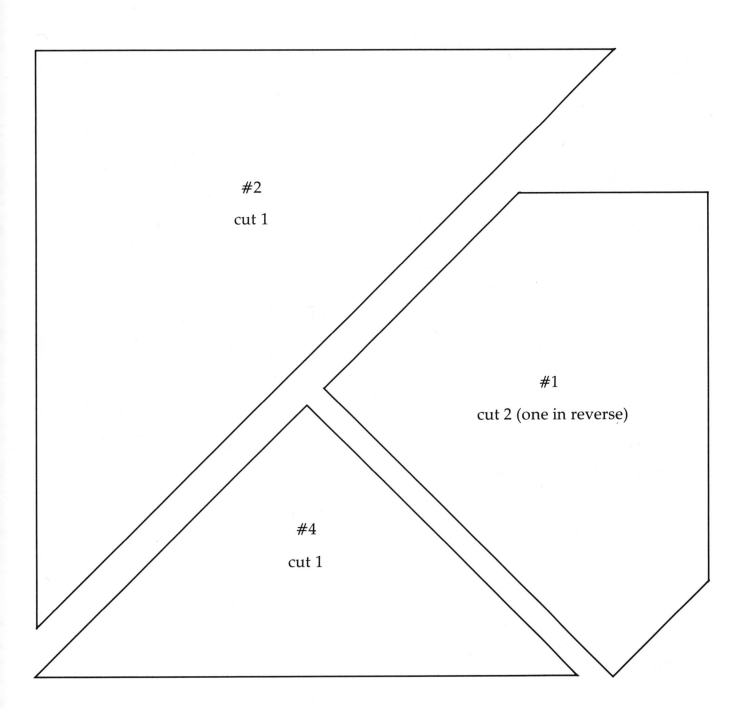

#2

cut 1

#1

cut 2 (one in reverse)

#4

cut 1

Card Trick

Nevada

Material
(45-inch-wide fabric)
⅓ yard red calico (A)
⅓ yard blue calico (B)
½ yard white solid (C)
½ yard gray solid (D)
½ yard navy blue solid (E)
1⅛ yards backing fabric
batting

Cut the following:
(includes ¼-inch seam allowance)
red calico
    8 squares 4¾ × 4¾ inches—cut into 2
       triangles each
    4 squares 5¼ × 5¼—cut into 4 triangles each
blue calico
    8 squares 4¾ × 4¾ inches—cut into 2
       triangles each
    4 squares 5¼ × 5¼ inches—cut into 4
       triangles each
white solid
    8 squares 4¾ × 4¾ inches—cut into 2
       triangles each
    4 squares 5¼ × 5¼ inches—cut into 4
       triangles each
    1 piece—cut in shape of state
gray solid
    2 pieces 1⅝ × 34¼ inches (top and bottom
       borders)
    2 pieces 1⅝ × 36½ inches (side borders)
    8 squares 4¾ × 4¾ inches—cut into 2
       triangles each
    4 squares 5¼ × 5¼ inches—cut into 4
       triangles each
navy solid
    16 squares 4¾ × 4¾ inches—cut into 2
       triangles each
    8 squares 5¼ × 5¼ inches—cut into 4
       triangles each

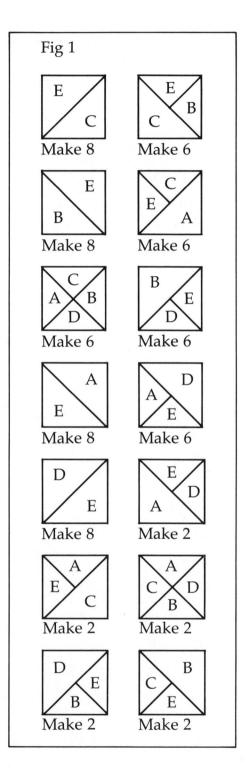

Fig 1

Make 8   Make 6
Make 8   Make 6
Make 6   Make 6
Make 8   Make 6
Make 8   Make 2
Make 2   Make 2
Make 2   Make 2

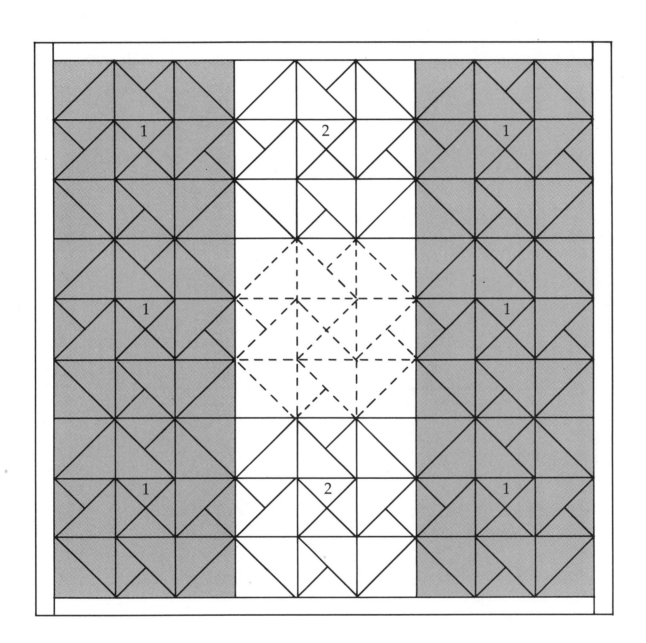

Directions

1. Join triangles to make squares according to Figure 1.
2. Join squares to make blocks (Figure 2).
3. Appliqué shape of state onto gray square (see page 117).
4. Join 3 blocks to make a row. Make 3 rows with the state block in the center. Or, replace center block with card trick (see diagram).
5. Join rows.
6. Join top and bottom border pieces to quilt top. Next, join sides.

To finish, see page 119.

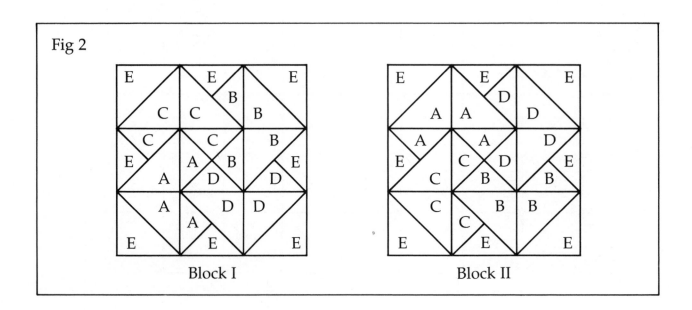

Fig 2

Block I   Block II

166

Alaska

Alaskan Winter

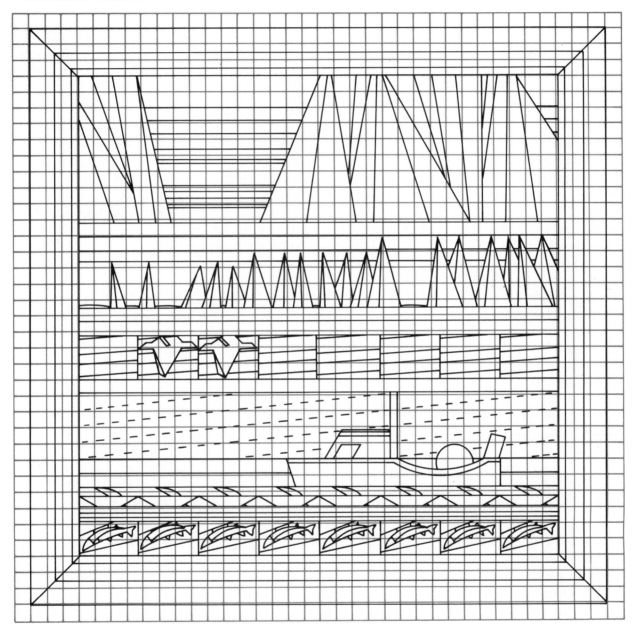

Each square equals 1 inch. To enlarge and transfer designs, see page 116. For appliqué instructions, see page 117.

167

Color Squares
California

Materials
(45-inch-wide fabric)
¼ yard white solid (A)
small amounts:
    pale yellow solid (B)
    yellow solid (C)
    mustard solid (D)
    light orange solid (E)
    orange solid (F)
    dark orange solid (G)
    red solid (H)
    navy blue solid (I)
    royal blue solid (J)
    blue solid (K)
    light blue solid (L)
    sky blue solid (M)
    light green solid (N)
    green solid (O)
    dark green solid (P)
    dard brown solid (Q)
    brown solid (R)
    light brown solid (S)
⅓ yard tan solid (T)
1⅛ yards backing fabric
batting

Cut the following:
(includes ¼-inch seam allowance)
white
    26 squares 2¼ × 2¼ inches
    15 squares 2¾ × 2¾ inches—cut into 2
        triangles each
solids (B through S)
    13 squares 2¼ × 2¼ inches
    1 square 2¾ × 2¾ inches—cut into 2
        triangles (use 1 triangle)
tan solid (T)
    13 squares 2¼ × 2¼ inches
    1 square 2¾ × 2¾ inches—cut into 2
        triangles (use 1 triangle)

2 border pieces 1⅝ × 29½ inches (sides)
2 border pieces 4 × 36½ inches (top and
    bottom)

Directions
1. Join squares in sequence according to diagram, to make rows (triangles are joined at each end of each row).
2. Next, join all rows (squares are on the diagonal).
3. Join side border strips and then join top and bottom border strips.
To finish, see page 119.

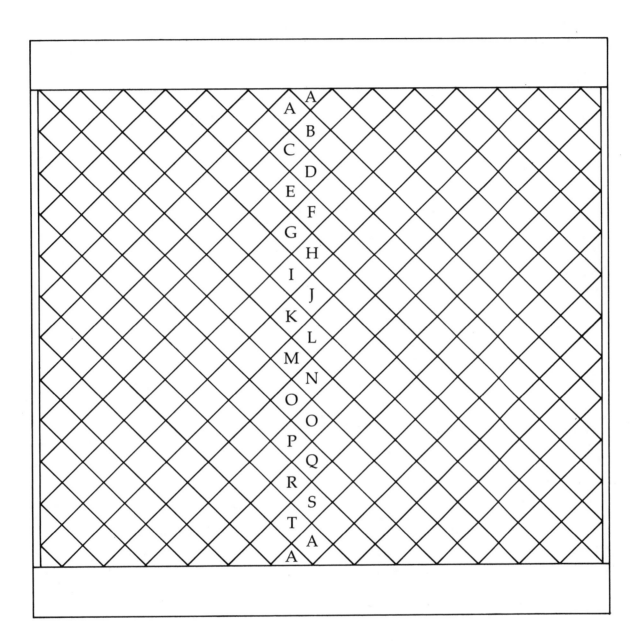

Participants in the Quilt Banner Project

Alabama

Bauer, Helen
Coleman, Gertrude
Deas, Dot
Edwards, Myrvelle
Fernandes, Barbara
Gibbons, Mel
Gwin, Lola
Haynie, Katherine
Kempter, Jeanette
Lazenby, Edna
Lazenby, Ethel
Leeth, La Tonya
Oden, Marsha
Sanford, Edna
Tankersley, Marilee
Ward, Mildred

Alaska

Cassidy, Beth
Chinn, Ramona
Renfrew, Mary

Arizona

Allen, Cindy
Amalong, Kay
Burchard, Lydia
Daniel, Nancy Brenan
Davidson, Valeria
Foster, Barbara
Fritzinger, Anna
Heatley, Elaine
Heidingsfelder, Sharon
Jaussaud, Janet
Kroggel, Phyllis
Lindenfeld, Mary Lynne
Ness, Ann Van
Phillips, Kathy
Phillips, Victoria

Rector, June
Reedy, Jeri A.
Sacker, Paula
Taylor, Linda

Arkansas

Adkins, Ruth
Agent, Betty Archer
Allen, Bernice
Ashcraft, Era
Larson, Lois
Lunsford, Judy
Parks, Jane
Pittman, Inona
Rickman, Mavis
Rushing, Virginia
White, Gladys

California

Brough, Charlotte
Creighton, Jeanne
Friebertshauser, Donna
Graf, Janet
Graf, Kimberley
Landrum, Juanita
Long, Sandra
Maranto, Sarah M.
O'Dell, Linda
Stool, Lindy
Verbrugghe, Kris

Colorado

Abrams, Lori
Adamson, Adrian
Ball, Elizabeth
Bloxsom, Mary
Briggs, Elinor
Bunn, Penny
Bunton, Craig

Challacombe, Ruth
Clemons, Kathy
Fisherbaugh, Melissa
Fowler, Charly
Frey, Opal
Hobby, Tiffany
Hollenback, Melanie
Johnson, Seth
Krimmer, Lisa
Leach, Lora
Lundberg, Suzanne
Neilsen, Diane
Parks, David
Reschke, Pam
Saulman, Sally
Staab, June
Tansey, Virginia
Tully, Mary
Watters, Joey
Watterson, Kimi
Weaver, Geoff
Wilson, Kierstin

Connecticut

Brown, Corinna
Pollock, Joan

Delaware

Andre, Pat
Brittingham, Mildred
Downs, Dorothy G.
Duvall, Jane
Epperly, Catherine
Grier, Mary
Hertzenberg, Virgene
Hook, Joan
Hook, Norina
Kozicki, Irene
Layton, Mary Sue

Manning, Brenda
Pie, Jeanette
Riddagh, Anne
Rodney, Mary Alice
Shaw, Alberta
Smith, Betty
Vaughn, Sylvia
Whittaker, Roxane

Florida

Amant, Carolyn St.
Gaffrey, Anna Marie
Martin, Myree Beck
Rasmussen, Shirley
Weller, Mary Frances
West, Harriet
Woods, Helen

Georgia

Berg, Alice
Clements, Doris B.
Johnson, Sylvia
Von Holt, Mary Ellen

Guam

Dunn, Gail

Hawaii

Nakama, Susan Bushell
Stewart, Janet

Idaho

Anderson, Alice
Branch, Bernice
Brewington, Leah
Caldwell, Willa
Davidson, Mary
Fronk, Kathy
Grubb, Shirley
Jenson, Glenda

Jones, Mrs.
Lanesky, Berdell
McDaniel, Helen
Naugler, Norma
Nilsson, Shirley
Richards, Evelyn
Sparbs, Sharon
Thomas, Faye
Wenders, Barbara

Illinois

Blank, Gerry
Burmeister, Mildred
Miller, Lisa
Miller, Mona
Pasley, Ellen
Schou, Betty

Indiana

Althaus, Carolyn
Cross, Marie
Doerstler, Pat
Hochstedler, Pat
Lee, Jean
Lienhart-Cross, Mary Ann
Marshall, Elizabeth
Pitman, Louise
Prather, Ruth
Weber, Juanita

Iowa

Danzer, Mary
Follett, Elizabeth
Follett, Patricia
George, Eillene
Kaltenheuser, Theresa
Knutson, Carolee
Schlichte, Ardella
Tribuno, Bertha Reth

Kansas

Bly, Myrtle
Brimmer, Sally
Brinkman, Dorothy
Brown, Suzanne
Burris, Joyce
Burton, Kathy
Carroll, Cathy
Cherry, Esther
Christie, Kimy
Craft, Elaine
Donaldson, Lois A.
Dungan, Lorraine
Edgerton, Amy
Edgerton, Cindi
Ferris, Una
Finnell, Ruth
French, Jane
Gillette, Diana
Goetz, Rose Mary
Groene, Dorothy
Hadachek, Katherine
Hagerman, Betty J.
Haines, Dorothy
Hand, Gail L.
Hansen, Martha
Harr, Martha
Hembrey, Denise
Hornback, Nancy
Huff, Polly
Johnson, AnneMarie
Johnson, Theresa
Kramer, Barbara
Kuehnle, Nancy
Lamb, Virginia
Lane, Diane
Lawson, Ann

Malone, Eleanor
Martz, Anita
Martz, Chelsea
McCarthy, Diane
McCray, Norma
McGowan, Lori
McIntosh, Lorraine
Monroe, Jan
Morris, Alice
Munson, Lynn
Neff, Melba
Nye, Jenny
Peternel, Ginger
Ray, Hilda
Rexroat, Phil
Richards, Karen
Rist, Linda
Roedell, Floyd
Roedell, Mary Lou
Schwarz, Ann
Seyfert, Bev
Simonds, Sigrid
Steiner, Marge
Stelovich, Maxine
Stewart, Aletha
Talamantez, Deb
Thompson, Shirley
Tolbert, Patricia V.
Walker, Kay
Walker, Pam
Ward, Donna
Webb, Lillie M.
Wettstaed, Sue
Woodruff, Carol
Woodworth, Carol

Kentucky

Ames, Gillian
Clark, Wayne
Combs, Chris
Evans, Ellen
Hallenberg, Shea
Hoge, Sara

Jackson, Reatha
Kaiser, Starr
Lorch, Kelley
Metzger, Christy
Morgan, Opal
Mucker, Stephanie
Palmer, Helen
Risse, Sandra
Sears, Ellen
Sebor, Bozena

Louisiana

Beaubouef, Patsy
Brown, Rita
Bullock, Lois
Cooper, Rosa
Haffner, Dora
Hague, Pat
Halbert, Pauline
Krotzer, Helma
Owen, Carla
Tricor, Sue H.

Maine

Babbidge, Judy
Beeler, Janice
Bennett, Juanita
Capen, Marjorie Weith
Crowel, Lillian H.
Curtis, June
Elwell, Mary
Ford, Louise
Gaudreau, Patience
Goddard, Julie
Heath, Maureen
Jones, Margaret
Knapp, Rose
Swazey, Lorraine
Swazey, Terry

Maryland

Calloway, Mary Beth
Clark, Vickey Lee Covey

Etzler, Laura
Jones, Patricia Kelley
Sexton, Mary
Skarda, Alice
Zudal, Pat

Massachusetts

Brown, Martha
Butler, Alice
Meyer, Connie
Morris, Judy
Troy, Diane E.

Michigan

Baker, Ann
Bateman, Janet
Bograff, Helen
Brady, Agnes
Cahoon, Karen
Cahoon, Zelma
Dalimonte, Lorraine
Derosha, Waunetta
Feighner, Maxine
Howarder, Ruth Ellen
Lodden, Blanche
Moliter, Mabel
Noel, Mary
Person, Carolyn
Sundell, Madalynn
Winkel, Susan Kay

Minnesota

Adleman, Carol
Eissinger, Yvonne
Fick, Ada
Johnson, Clare
Kuehl, Edde
Kyllo, Dorrie
Lang, Susie
Lehrke, Sandy
Maltry, Mary Ellen
Rock, Yvonne
Saign, Muriel

Smith, Char
Smith, Dorothy
Stein, Susan
Uhlman, Bette Lou

Mississippi

Adair, Louise
O'Reilly, Louise
Richardson, Mrs. Chalmers
Strain, Mrs. Derwood
Webb, Mrs. Eugene F.

Missouri

Barto, Gladys
Benson, Joan
Conners, Bobby
Cox, Arvilla
Davis, Mary
Graham, Sandra
Green, Margie
Harlan, Lolita
Johnson, Virginia
Kasper, Ruth
Lammert, Ethel
Mayberry, Sydney
Overby, Ronnie
Plackemeier, Verna
Schroeder, Margaret
Segur, Arlene
Shull, Dorothy
Sparkman, Mike
Wappelhorst, Jeanette
Yates, Juanita
Yates, Nancy

Montana

Chaffey, Geneva
Huston, Suzanne
Rieger, Elsie
Searl, Gail
Van Haur, Shelley
Vosen, Karen
York, Emma

Nebraska

Heeren, Marian

Nevada

Corica, Sherrie
Dupree, Elsie
Shipley, Leota
Sylvester, Emma
Turner, Clemmie
Warner, Goldie

New Hampshire

Ash, Jill
Bailey, Joanne
Barnes, Lynda
Beal, Margaret
Bean, Dot
Beauchamp, Sue
Bickford, Susan
Blaisdell, Nicole
Bresse, Ami
Bugnacki, Liz
Carozza, Jean
Chase, Nancy
Clark, Mona
Doak, Carol
Downs, Cathie
Downs, Mary Anne
DuBois, Bonnie
Flanders, Lois
Forand, Margaret
Fourler, Karen
Goodnow, Marcia
Greenwood, Nancy
Guillemette, Susan
Gynan, Liza
Hancock, Janis
Harding, Adrienne
Hatch, Sandra
Hatch, Sandy
Hersey, Clarabelle
Hubbard, Nancy
Ide, Beth J.

Ilsley, Davideen
Inglis, Carolyn
Jewett, Wanda
Jones, Martha
Keenan, Susan
Kelley, Gail
Kelley, Mary
Kincaid, Michele O.
King, Karen
Knowlton, Dawn
Kurzban, Claire
Labanaris, Faye
Levesque, Susan
MacDonald, Madeline
McGairy, Penny
McKone, Jessie
Owen, Carol
Paone, Robin
Pearson, Pam
Peterson, Lois
Pike, Doris
Powierza, Kelly
Raban, Susan
Redmond, Wen
Riddle, Michelle
Scherf, Linda
Schulte, Nan
Scruton, Pauline
Sheldon, Debbie
Standish, Jeannie
Swasey, Ruth
Tibbetts, Tracie
Tuttle, Linda
Wallace, Marilynn
White, Ann
Williams, Kay

New Jersey

Cassidy, Bettylou
MacConnell, Lynn
Madsen, Joan
Rindge, Jeanette
Thomas, Marci

New Mexico

Collins, Janet Wetzig
Constantine, Dolores
Fellmeth, Jean
Frizzell, Juanice
Haddock, Mary
Malcolm, Jane
Mozer, Marilyn
Spiullman, Trish

New York

Bachraty, Alice M.
Berg, Jaqueline
Bliss, Tina
Brehmer, Margaret
Brown, Leola
Cerny, Helen
Cerny, Sharon
Colucci, Mary
Concepcion, Naomi
Conry, Kathleen
Cooper, Marion
Cross, Linda
Curtin, Liz
Evans, Jane T.
Goldsmith, Susan
Haresign, Marlene
Hotaling, Muriel
Hurwich, Susan Lori
John, Diana
Kagen, Laure
Kovacik, Helen
Kravitz, Patricia
Macosko, Sharon
Maher, Marlene
Nash, Lois
Nash, Paul
Noble, Keturah
Page-Kessler, Janet
Quinn, Leslie
Rausch, Mary
Rodio, Carla

Schwartz, Kathy
Sico, Robin
Stibitz, Marguerite
Stires, Barbara
Stover, Alice
Tuitt, Agnes
Tukufu, Quassia
Waclawski, Gary

North Carolina

Baker, Gladys
Carr, Sara
Goodman, Nancy Stroupe

North Dakota

Dissette, Maxine
Falk, Sara
Filler, Darleen
Hinderer, Hilda
Hoger, Helen
Holle, Florence
Myers, Bertha
Odegaard, Carol
Olson, Cheryl
Reis, Irene
Swanson, Joan
Thompson, Esther
Tjon, Alphild
VanErem, Shirlee
Wahl, Sara
Will, Agnes

Ohio

Dawson, Peggy
Emmert, Ruth Ann
Gardiner, Louise
Hanson, Elsie
Hartman, Helen
Hinden, Judee
Hoy, Barbara
Hunt, Ivadel
Hyme, Lucile
Jones, Ferne

Lockwood, Thelma
McDougall, Barbara
McGlone, Martha
Miller, Patricia
Mooter, Mary
Probasco, Janet
Shawhan, Rosemary
Stokes, Kim
Strahler, Mrs. Kenneth
Wilkins, Vashti

Oklahoma

Codopony, Patty
De Mond, Lois
Gaylor, Zola
Montgomery, Ruth
Rose, Sue
Sharp, Gladys
Strickland, Deborah P.

Oregon

Blaire, Phillis
Burgard, Roxy
Margason, Ingrid
Meyers, Carole
Peters, Audrey
Smith, Delila

Pennsylvania

Sacks, Shirley
White, Fannie

Rhode Island

Cullinan, Dawn Lyon
Dipina, Elizabeth
Feeley, Kathy
Hilliard, Linda
King, Deborah
King, Irene
Little, Barbara
Luke, Anna
Motta, Anthony J.
Motta, Elsie M.

Poor, Yvette
Wise, Mary

South Carolina

Attaway, Patsy
Barton, Gwen
Bedenbaugh, LaBruce
Berley, Peggy
Boozer, Mildred
Brigman, Evelyn
Bussey, Marie
Cox, Mary Ruth
Crapps, Ruth
Davenport, Jerry
Dominick, Ophelia
Duncan, Grace
Ivey, Edna
Long, Gloria
McCollum, Jill
Schedler, Ursula
Weaver, Barbara
Wiseman, Sally

South Dakota

Diehl, Dawn
Finck, Margorie
Impecoven, Ella
Jensen, Luanne
Patterson, Esther
Seibel, Beverly
Teachout, Darlene
Vanderboom, Nancy

Tennessee

Anthony, Carol
Anthony, Elaine
Anthony, Paul
Cole, Joyce
Idol, Faye
Joy, Edmund J.
Kestner, Freddie
Manning, Edwina
Meier, Bettylu
Rebello, Kay

Texas

Chick, Nancy
Harvey, Bonnie
Johnston, Barbara
Larson, Florence Lois
Massa, Marilyn
Murphy, Anita
Musgrove, Ellen
Stein, Helen
Wilson, Shirley

Utah

Boerens, Trice
Buehler, Jo
Noyes, Linnea
Olson, Rebecca
Scott, Linda Jean

Vermont

Fitch, Earlene

Virginia

Adams, Susie Spencer
Beery, Mary
Chaney, Wileina
Chappell, Helen
Fisher, Hazel
Foskett, Patricia
Hanneman, Kay
Heatwole, Margaret
Hockman, Margie
Maxey, Dancey
Shibut, Ann

Washington

Alton, Lu
Brydson, Betsi
Coombs, Diane
Karlinsey, Cathern
Park, Jerry
Parks, Betty
Sonderland, Alberta
Whitney, Alta

West Virginia

Ford, Sharon
Masters, Bonnie
Moran, Juanita
Parcell, Judy

Wisconsin

Baker, Jeanne
Bennett, Kathy
Carriere, Linda
Dahlke, Margarete
Folz, Darlene
Jones, Joanna
Ketter, Keryl
Knack, Peggy
Lundberg, Jody
Lundy, Linda
Mills, Robin
Nevins, Doreen
Rosen, Evie
Sorenson, Fran
Tetzlaff, Audrey
Vieaux, Geri
Vogel, Mary
Wild, Marge
Wurman, Arlene

Wyoming

Adams, Elizabeth
Airheart, Nora
Albee, Jan
Anderson, Agnes
Barfels, Kathy
Big Piney, H.S. H.E. class
Bixby, Betty
Boley, Pam
Bradley, Deanne
Burkhardt, Dottie
Burleson, Elissa
Butler, Iva
Caldwell, Jewell
Caroll, Dorothy
Cesko, Doris

Cunningham, Esther
Dorsett, Reba
Duvall, Esther
Ellis, Cathy
Freeburg, Helen
Geneveux, Mary
Graham, Edna Mae
Graham, Nancy
Grover, LuAnn
Hecox, Dorothy
Helmer, Elsie
Hemsher, Cathy
Henberg, Agnes
Henry, Karen
Henry, Anna May
Henry, Carma Jean
Herder, Katie
Hobson, Lorna
Hoffman, Betty
Hovda, Betty
Hulten, Linda

Hunt, Jackie
Hunziker, Bonnie
Jacobsen, Virginia
James, Emma
James, Hazel
Jepson, Evelyn
Kidman, Louise
Littlewind, Carol
Lybyer, Mable
Maxfield, Dot
McWilliams, Madge
Miller, Alice
Munns, Cheryl
Neal, Diane
Newlin, Terry
Omundson, Terry
Overman, Wyona
Padget, Gayle
Peterson, Lois
Rahm, Jean

Rich, Fern
Roberts, Betty
Rogers, Mary
Samuelson, Pam
Schell, Berenice
Schell, Tanya
Schneider, Donna
Schultz, Deb
Smith, Bobbie
Smith, Florence
Snapp, Anita
Strohmaeir, Loreene
Swanson, Patty
Thelmar, Hattie
Vickrey, Linda
Walker, Berenice
Wall, Edna
Wall, Freda
White, Jessie
Whittaker, Myrtle